CROWOOD SPORTS GUIDES
HOCKEY
SKILLS • TECHNIQUES • TACTICS

Jane Powell

THE CROWOOD PRESS

First published in 2009 by
The Crowood Press Ltd
Ramsbury, Marlborough
Wiltshire SN8 2HR

www.crowood.com

British Library Cataloguing-in-Publication Data
A catalogue record for this book is available from the British Library.

ISBN 978 1 84797 122 7

Disclaimer
Please note that the author and the publisher of this book are not responsible, or liable, in
any manner whatsoever, for any damage, or injury of any kind, that may result from practising,
or applying, the techniques and methods and/or following the instructions described in this
publication. Since the exercises and other physical activities described in this book may be too
strenuous in nature for some readers to engage in safely, it is essential that a doctor is consulted
before undertaking such exercises and activities.

Acknowledgements
The author and publishers would like to thank the following for their help in the production
of this book: Jessica Brooker, JAB Photography, for the photographs (except where credited
otherwise), and the GB Youth Squad for their practical demonstrations.

Typeset by Bookcraft, Stroud, Gloucestershire
Printed and bound in Malaysia by Times Offset (M) Sdn Bhd

CONTENTS

DEDICATION

To my friends Pip, Pete, Andrew and Ben Gardner, with thanks for their patience, fun and help in the writing of this book.

PREFACE

Hockey is a fun, fast and skilful team game. It is a stick and ball game with its origins dating back thousands of years. It is also an Olympic sport and as such is one of the few team sports in the Olympics. For the majority of people hockey is a family sport that can be played by young and old alike. It has moved over the centuries from a female sport played on grass to a mixed gender sport played on artificial turf pitch. Hockey is a game that has been played in a number of schools and is one of the invasion games that can be played as part of the National Curriculum.

Hockey can be traced back to the earliest civilizations of the world, but the modern game of field hockey was developed in the British Isles, and started around the mid-1800s as an alternative to football for cricketers who wanted to practise a winter sport. The game has developed greatly since when it was played with a rubber cube rather than a ball. The rules of hockey are very similar to the rules of football except that players must use sticks instead of their feet to play the ball, and in hockey there is no offside rule. Top level hockey is played almost exclusively on artificial grass or water-based pitches, which has made it a fast, energetic and exciting game to watch.

Although hockey will differ slightly in its set-up between the various countries where it is played, the core skills and tactical applications will be the same. A variation of the game is indoor hockey where most of the skills are transferable from the outdoor game; the only skill that is not allowed is the hit and long-handled sweep.

The aim of this book is to improve the ability in hockey of all readers, young or old, novice or expert. Through a series of chapters that are easy to read and understand, the sport of hockey is explained, and explanation is also given of the techniques and skills necessary to playing a game of hockey and competing at your chosen level. There is advice on training, nutrition and where to play to help you whether you play at club, regional or international level.

Ashley Jackson evading the oncoming Indian defender. GB v India, 6 March 2008, Olympic Qualifiers, Chile. (Photograph supplied by England Hockey, source unknown)

PART I
INTRODUCTION TO HOCKEY

CHAPTER I

THE HISTORY OF HOCKEY

Games with curved sticks and a ball have been played throughout history and in various regions of the world. In Egypt there are 4,000-year-old drawings of the game being played. Hurling dates back to before 1272BC, and there are illustrations from 500BC, in Ancient Greece. There were various hockey-like games played throughout Europe during the Middle Ages, and the word 'hockey' was recorded in the Galway Statutes of 1527.

The modern game of hockey grew from the game played in English public schools in the early nineteenth century. The first club was created in 1849 at Blackheath in south-east London, but the modern rules grew out of a version of hockey played by members of Middlesex Cricket Clubs for winter sport.

The Hockey Association was founded in 1886 and the first match was held between England and Ireland on 16 March 1895 at Richmond Hockey Club. England finished as 5–0 victors. The International Rules Board was founded in 1900.

Hockey was played at the summer Olympics in 1908 and 1920. It was dropped from the games by the organizing committee in 1924, leading to the foundation of the Fédération Internationale de Hockey sur Gazon (the FIH) as an international governing body by seven continental European nations. Hockey was reinstated to

England Men in the early 1900s. (Photograph supplied by England Hockey, source unknown)

the Olympic Games in 1928, and in 1970, men's hockey was united under the FIH.

The game had been introduced to India by British servicemen, and the first clubs formed in Calcutta in 1885. The Beighton Cup and the Aga Khan tournament had commenced within ten years. Entering the Olympic Games in 1928, India won all five of its games without conceding a goal, and went on to win in 1932 until 1956, and then in 1964 and 1980. Pakistan won in 1960, 1968 and 1984.

In the early 1970s, artificial turf fields began to be used in competitions. The introduction of synthetic pitches to replace grass has completely changed most aspects of hockey. The game, as well as the material used to play, has taken a definitive turn, transforming the game, gaining mainly in speed. In order to take into account the specificities of this surface, new tactics and new techniques have been developed, often followed by the establishment of new rules to take account of these techniques. The switch to synthetic surfaces essentially ended Indian and Pakistani domination of the sport. Artificial turf is far more costly than grass, and too expensive for the two countries to introduce widely in comparison to the wealthier European countries. From the 1970s Australia, The Netherlands and Germany have dominated the sport at the Olympics.

Women do not seem to have played hockey widely before the modern era. Women's hockey was first played at British universities and schools, and the first club, Moseley Ladies Hockey Club, was founded in 1887. The first national association was the Irish Ladies Hockey Union in 1894, and although rebuffed by the Hockey Association, Women's hockey grew rapidly around the world. This led to the formation of the International Federation of Women's Hockey Associations (IFWHA) in 1927. Initially this did not include many continental European countries where women played as sections of Men's Hockey Associations and were affiliated to the FIH. The IFWHA held conferences every three years, and the tournaments associated with these were the primary IFWHA competitions. These tournaments were non-competitive until 1975.

By the early 1970s there were 22 associations with women's sections in the FIH and 36 associations in the IFWHA. Discussions were started about a common rule book. The FIH introduced competitive tournaments in 1974, forcing the acceptance of the principle of competitive hockey by the IFWHA in 1973. It took until 1982 for the two bodies to merge, but this allowed the introduction of women's hockey to the Olympic Games from 1980 where, as in the men's game, The Netherlands, Germany and Australia have been consistently strong.

The game of hockey is played widely across the world. In England it is a popular family orientated sport, played mainly in clubs by both men and women. The game is well liked in many schools, particularly in the independent sector and offers a lifetime of both sporting and social opportunities for players, officials and administrators alike.

Hockey, or field hockey as it is also known to differentiate it from ice hockey, is an eleven-a-side game played on a pitch 91.4m × 55m (100yd × 60yd) with a ball of 23cm (9in) circumference. Each player has a stick with a rounded head to play the ball with the ultimate aim of scoring goals by putting the ball in the other team's goal. Sticks are about a metre long and weigh 340g–790g (12–28oz).

The rules of hockey are very similar to the rules of football except that players must use sticks instead of their feet to play the ball. There are eleven players on a team made up of a goalkeeper, defenders, midfielders and attackers. The only player on the field who is allowed to use their feet and hands as well as their stick is the goalkeeper. Chapter 2 provides a comprehensive explanation of the rules.

In England and the rest of the UK the season lasts from September until May.

The History of the Game in England

The origins of the game can be traced back to the earliest civilizations of the world, but the modern game of field

hockey was developed in the British Isles. The modern game was started in England in the mid-1800s as an alternative to football for cricketers seeking a winter sport.

The first organized club was the Blackheath Football and Hockey Club, which dates back to at least 1861. Another London club, at Teddington, helped refine the game by introducing a number of the modern rules and concepts, including the introduction of a spherical ball, which replaced a rubber cube. Most importantly, they instituted the striking circle, which was incorporated into the rules of the newly-founded Hockey Association (men's) in London in 1886. The All England Women's Hockey Association was then founded in 1895, becoming the first women's national sporting governing body.

The game spread throughout the British Empire, largely with the British army and this is one reason why India, Pakistan and Australia are so formidable, as all were once British colonies. Today, field hockey is played all over the world by a variety of countries and field hockey is currently recognized as the second largest team sport in the world, after football.

The International Game

The first men's international match was held between England and Ireland on 16 March 1895 at Richmond Hockey Club, with England finishing as 5–0 victors. The women played their first official international match on 2 March 1896 when they travelled to Dublin to compete against Ireland. The Irish team won the match 2–0 with both goals coming in the first half.

Men's field hockey first featured in the London Olympics of 1908 but the women's game was not introduced to the Olympics until the Moscow Games of 1980. The highlight for the British game in modern times was an Olympic gold medal for the men in 1988 (Seoul, South Korea). It was the third time gold had been achieved; other successes came in 1908 (London) and 1920 (Antwerp). The British women's team won a bronze medal at the 1992 games (Barcelona).

England Women in the early 1900s. (Photograph supplied by England Hockey, source unknown)

The Men's World Cup was introduced in 1971. England's best success to date in the World Cup came in 1986 when the men finished with a silver medal after losing 2–1 to Australia in the final, hosted on home soil at Willesden. The women won the International Federation of Women's Hockey Associations (IFWHA) tournament against Wales in 1975 (Edinburgh), the tournament that preceded the World Cup, which was introduced in 1979.

For many years the women played an annual international fixture at Wembley Stadium, regularly attracting over 50,000 spectators. The first international at Wembley was held in 1951 when England beat Ireland 6–1. March 1978 saw a record-breaking crowd of 65,000 packed into Wembley to watch England draw 2–2 with the USA.

Clubs representing England in Europe have also enjoyed success, most recently with Reading winning the 2003 Men's European Club Championships in a nail-biting final where they came from 1–0 down to take the game to penalty strokes, emerging as eventual winners. Olton and West Warwickshire achieved a silver medal in the 2003 Women's European Club Championships losing out to Den Bosch in the final.

Throughout the history of hockey, the main factor in shaping the game we know today came from experimenting with the rules. Hockey began as an eleven-a-side game, with two substitutes. In 1927, the need for two umpires was recognized, with each umpire looking after each half of the pitch. In 1949 the radius of the shooting circle became sixteen yards,

although this was not introduced into the women's game until nearly twenty years later. The penalty stroke as we know it today, replaced the penalty bully in 1963, followed shortly afterwards by the sideline hit replacing the sideline roll in.

One of the more interesting rules was the use of a hand. Up until 1983, the use of a hand was permitted. This was then abolished and applied to all players apart from the goalkeeper. Around the same time, umpires were given three cards to use as warnings and to serve suspensions (see Chapter 2).

Probably the most significant change and influence on today's game occurred in 1992 – with significantly more impact in 2007 – when the rules changed to allow a team to remove a goalkeeper and play with eleven outfield players. Having an extra outfield player obviously gives a greater attacking advantage, but this has to be weighed up with the risk of having no goalkeeper, should the team concede a penalty corner, for example. This has not been used frequently in higher level games, but it is an exciting rule to watch out for in the future.

There have been changes other than in the rules that have influenced the game as we know it. We have already mentioned that changes in playing surface affected the game greatly. In 2007/08, the Euro Hockey League in its inaugural year tried and tested some interesting new rules and structures to the game. The greatest difference is the introduction of timed quarters. The teams were given two extra breaks to discuss tactics, formations and so on. This leads to an exciting change in the approach to the game, with tactics being changed more regularly as a team chased a goal, or tried to protect a positive scoreline.

The second most notable change, and probably the most exciting from the point of view of the spectator, was that of the seven-second penalty stroke, whereby a stroke is usually taken from a static position. The Euro League rules stated that the attacker would start on the 25yd line, and would have seven seconds to go one-on-one against the goalkeeper – similar to the rules of ice hockey. This proved to be a great success, and these rulings may be ones to look out for in the future. Many other competitions experiment with the rules, and report back to the FIH as to how the rulings worked. These trials may well see a whole new set of rules in the future. Who would have thought twenty years ago, for example, that hockey would ever discontinue the offside rule?

It is estimated that over three million people, on five continents, play field hockey. It is the second largest team sport after football in the world, and the largest mixed sport in England. Since 1992, with the introduction of rolling substitutes and squads of sixteen, the game has increased in intensity. International teams are now making between thirty and fifty substitutions per game. Defenders will stay on for longer periods of time but attackers and midfielders will play for 8–12 minutes and rotate, working at full speed and intensity. This substitution rule is one of the key reasons why the speed of the game has increased. Players have to be fitter and quicker to play the modern game.

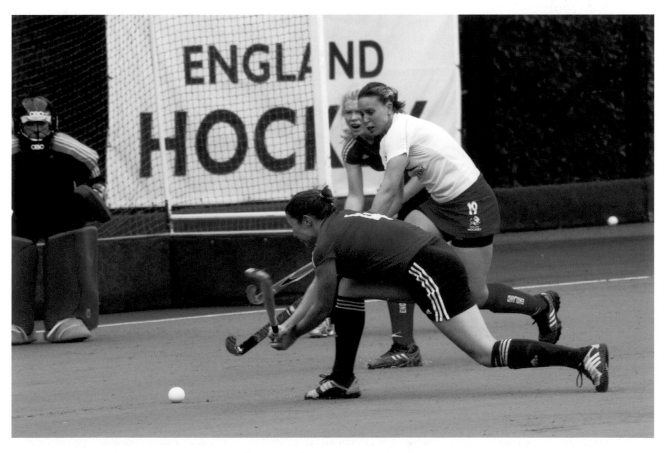

The game has moved on rapidly with the change of playing surface, equipment and clothing..

CHAPTER 2

RULES OF THE GAME

The Pitch

Most hockey field dimensions were originally fixed using whole numbers of imperial measures and these are shown in parenthesis. It is the metric measurements that are the current official dimensions of the field of play as laid down by the International Hockey Federation (FIH) in the *Rules of Hockey 2008*.

The game is played on a 91.4m × 55m (100 × 60yd) rectangular field. At each end there is a goal 2.14m (7ft) high and 3.66m (12ft) wide, and a semi-circle 14.63m (16yd) from the goal known as the shooting circle (or D or arc), with a dotted line 5m (5yds) from the semi-circle, as well as lines across the field 22.9m (25yd) from each endline and in the centre of the field. A spot, called the penalty spot, is placed 6.4m (7yd) from the centre of each goal.

The Rules of Play

Newcomers to hockey will need an introduction to the concepts and terms that will be used later (see also the Glossary at the end of the book).

Some Major Hockey Concepts

*   **Defending** is the act of protecting or defending the goal from the opposition.
*   **Evading** is the act of moving the ball away from the defenders to evade them and steal the ball. This can be by dribbling the ball or passing the ball.
*   **Pathways and channels** are imaginary lines drawn in relation to the goal that the players are moving towards.

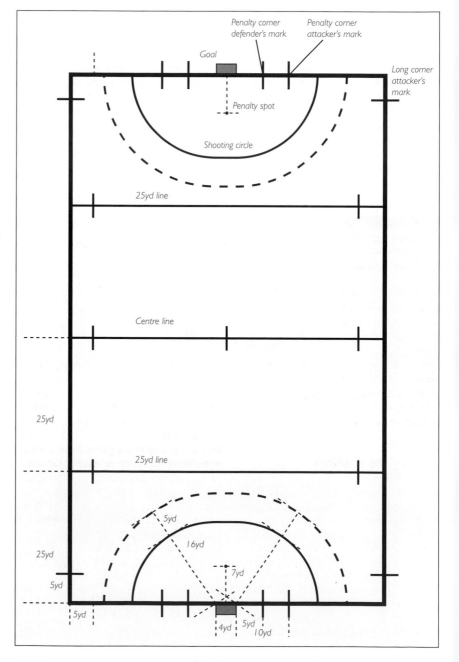

A field hockey pitch with markings.

- **Lines of defence** usually run across the pitch and are staggered so that the player with the ball cannot beat all the opposition with one move or pass.
- **Vision and scanning** both require the player to look up whilst moving around the pitch, either with or without the ball. The other aspect of vision and scanning is the ability to see the opposition players and which direction they are moving around the pitch.

Some Important Hockey Terms

- **Ball carry** and **dribble.** Both of these terms describe moving up the pitch with the ball in contact with and under control of the stick.
- **The wing** is an area of the pitch down the side, and a player there is 'on the wing'. A **winger** is operating in the area down the side of the pitch.

Hockey is a fast, skilful and exciting team game. The teams are each made up of sixteen players, but the rules of the game permit only eleven to be on the field at any one time. One of the eleven must be a goalkeeper. No game of hockey can be played unless each team has a goalkeeper on the field throughout the game. Each team member has a position and each position has a role to play.

Roles of the Positions

- Centre Forward (CF) is the player whose main role is to score goals.
- Right Inner (RI) and Left Inner (LI) play inside the two wings and support the CF, RW and LW to score goals.
- Right Wing (RW) and Left Wing (LW) give width in attack, cross the ball into the shooting area and score goals.
- Centre Half (CH) links the defence and attack; very much a central player, CH is used as a pivot in attack

and a defender when the opposition have the ball.
- Right Half (RH) and Left Half (LH) mark the opposition wings, are wide attackers and back up the forwards in attack.
- Right Back (RB) and Left Back (LB) mark the CF and cover for the rest of the team in defence.
- Goalkeeper (GK) stops the opposition scoring.
- Substitutes can play any of the above positions and will rotate regularly throughout the game as there is no limit to the number of substitutions that can be used.

Marking Opposing Players

As an attacking team you are trying to get past your opponent and score a goal. Each team member will be responsible for trying to prevent the player on the opposition team playing in the same position from dribbling the ball, or passing the ball past them, and preventing them from scoring a goal.

Substitution

There are sixteen players but only eleven can play at any one time, which leaves five substitutes for each team. They are known as rolling substitutes because they can enter the field of play, be taken off the field and put back on again. Normally they will all play in the game: there are no restrictions; the coach or teacher can use each substitute player as often as required. This rolling substitution helps to keep hockey fast and exciting. In fact England senior teams are doing 40–50 substitutions each game. It is a high intensity game (see Chapter 15, Physical Fitness).

What Players Should Not Do

Hockey players are encouraged to be skilful. Good ball and stick skills are essential.

Players are coached to move the ball in a variety of directions at speed. However, only the flat side of the stick can be used. Players must not use the rounded side of the stick.

It is an offence to propel the ball forward with any part of your body. It makes no difference if it is accidental or intentional: it is an offence and the umpire will blow the whistle.

It is also an offence to kick the ball or intentionally stop it with your foot. The only players who are allowed to kick the ball are the goalkeepers. As with the other offences, the umpire will blow the whistle immediately it happens.

It is an offence for any field player to play the ball with the stick at above shoulder height and if a player does so the umpire will blow the whistle and give a penalty to the other team. However, just like the kicking offence, the goalkeepers are allowed to play the ball with the stick at above shoulder height, as long as they do not endanger other players. Very often the goalkeeper will use a high stick to stop a shot on goal.

Stopping the Ball

As we have seen, it is an offence to kick the ball (with the exception of the goalkeepers) or use the rounded side of the stick. Every time this happens, the umpire will blow the whistle and award a penalty to the other team. A penalty could be a free-hit or a penalty corner or even a penalty stroke, depending on the circumstances and where on the field the incident took place. For example, if it was in the mid-field area, then it would be a free-hit; if it was a defender in the shooting circle, then it would be a penalty corner to the attack or, if it were an attacker in the shooting circle, then it would be a free-hit to the defence.

Dangerous Play

The rules of the game of hockey are also there to protect the players; they are very important because unless they are followed, play can be dangerous. Here are some rules that prevent dangerous play.

- Players must not hit each other with their sticks.
- Players must not trip each other or threaten each other.
- Players must not intentionally bash or clash sticks.
- Players must not raise the ball dangerously at each other.
- Players must not play the ball with the stick at above shoulder height (except the goalkeepers).

Goalkeepers

Goalkeepers are the only players allowed to kick the ball. However, they must not kick it when they are standing outside the shooting circle.

Goalkeeper's Equipment

A goalkeeper is allowed to wear protective equipment, which includes leg pads, kickers, hand protectors, body protector, elbow pads, shoulder pads and so on. In addition, a goalkeeper has a helmet that must be worn at all times, and a stick. There is more detail on goalkeeping equipment in Chapter 11.

The goalkeeper must not remove the helmet during the game unless he or she is taking a penalty stroke. Goalkeepers also wear a shirt of a different colour to the field players. This allows the players, the umpires and the spectators to see the goalkeepers clearly at all times. The shirt must be worn over the top of the protective equipment (that is, the body protector, shoulder pads and so on).

Scoring

There are three types of goal in hockey; they are:

- a field goal
- a penalty corner
- a penalty stroke.

Field Goal

A field goal is a goal scored from open, continuous play. Field goals may only be taken from the shooting circle, a roughly semi-circular area in front of the opponents' goal. If a ball is hit from outside the shooting circle and goes into the goal, it does not count as a goal.

Penalty Corner

If a defending team breaks certain rules, the other team may be awarded a penalty corner. Often (but not always) penalty corners are awarded because a team

breaks a rule while defending in their shooting circle.

To take a penalty corner, play is stopped to allow the teams to take their positions in attack and defence. One attacker stands with the ball on a designated spot on the backline. (This is the line that marks the shorter boundary of the field of play and on which the goal is placed.) This player will play (hit, push or drag) the ball to other attackers, waiting to take a shot at goal. The other attackers usually wait at the top of the shooting circle to receive the ball. But in any case, all attackers have to be outside the shooting circle until the penalty corner begins.

Up to five defenders (including the goalkeeper) position themselves behind

Goalkeeping equipment.

the backline (either inside or outside of the goal) to defend against the penalty corner. The rest of the defenders must stay behind the centre-line until the ball is played (until the penalty corner is taken).

To actually take the penalty corner, the ball is hit, pushed or dragged to the attacker waiting to receive it. Before a shot on goal can be taken, the ball must first pass outside the shooting circle. Once this has happened the receiver usually hits, pushes or deflects it back into the shooting circle for the first shot at goal.

If the first shot is a hit, as opposed to other types of shots, like a 'flick' or a 'scoop', the ball must enter into the goal at a height of no more than 460mm (18in). It is usually easy to tell if the ball is at the

right height since the board at the back of the goal is the same height.

When a goal is successfully scored, there is a familiar sound of the ball hitting the board, usually followed by players celebrating.

If the first shot is a 'scoop' or a 'flick' – shots that are lifted into the air and thus usually a little slower than a hit – then the ball can cross the goal-line at any height, as long as it is not dangerous play.

Once the attacker on the backline starts the corner (plays the ball), the defenders on the backline may move into the shooting circle, and do their best to keep the other team from scoring.

In practice this all happens very quickly, and can be exciting to watch.

Penalty Stroke

A penalty stroke is a shot taken on goal by a chosen player and defended only by the goalkeeper. (All other players must stand outside the circle, about 23m (25yd) back.) A penalty stroke may be awarded for a few reasons, the most common being an offence by a defender in the circle to prevent the probable scoring of a goal. The shot is taken from a spot 6.4m (7yd) directly in front of the goal. Match time is stopped when a penalty stroke is being taken.

Duration of a Match

A regulation length hockey match lasts for seventy minutes, broken into two halves of thirty-five minutes each. The team with the most goals at the end of the seventy minutes is the winner. It is also possible for a match to end in a draw (or a tie). But in some matches – like in a tournament such as the World Cup or Olympics, or in a championship game – you must have a winner. In those cases, a match that is tied at the end of regulation time then goes into extra time (the first team to score in extra time wins) and, if necessary, to a penalty stroke competition.

Umpires and Umpiring

All hockey matches have two umpires who work together to control the game. They are sometimes called 'the third team on the pitch'. They both wear the same colour shirt or sweater and one of them blows the whistle each time a player commits an offence.

Like the players, the umpires have their own hockey equipment. Essential umpiring equipment comprises:

* two whistles (one is a spare)
* a stopwatch to time the game
* pencil and paper to record each goal (the score) and the number of any player who receives a warning or a suspension

A goalkeeper saving a penalty stroke.

Free hit signal: one arm points in the direction of the free hit.

Sideline hit signal: one arm points down to the sideline and the other arm in the direction of the hit.

Penalty corner signal: both arms point toward the goal.

16 yard hit out signal: both arms extend horizontally.

Penalty stroke signal: one arm points to the ground and the other up to the sky.

Goal scored signal: both arms point to the halfway line.

- warning cards (green, yellow and red)
- a *Hockey Rules Book*
- an assortment of useful things such as string, scissors or a small penknife to repair any damage to goal nets, and so on.

Umpires blow the whistle to stop the game and make a signal to tell the players what the penalty is and what it was for. An example is a free-hit for pushing in the mid-field, or a penalty corner for an offence by the defence in the shooting circle.

Use of Coloured Cards

- A Green card is given as a warning to a player that they are not playing within the rules of the game.
- A Yellow card is given to a player as a temporary suspension of 5–10 minutes. If a player has already been given a green card and repeats an offence, or commits a foul that shows a lack of control, they will get a Yellow card.
- A Red card signals a more permanent suspension from the game and usually follows a serious offence that causes injury to the opposition. The length of the suspension depends on the national governing body.

Umpire's Signals

There are many umpire's signals, including the ones illustrated opposite.

There are two adaptations of field hockey, mini-hockey and quicksticks.

Mini-Hockey (seven-a-side game)

The Pitch

The pitch is only half the size of an eleven-a-side pitch and there are fourteen players as opposed to twenty-two players. There are no 23m lines; the penalty stroke spots

are closer to the goal-lines (5m instead of 7m) and the corner markers are closer to the corners (3m instead of 5m). The shooting circles, the penalty corner markers, goals and centre-line are all exactly the same.

The Rules of Play

There are three key differences from the eleven-a-side game.

- Any intentional offence by a player in their defending half of the pitch should be penalized by the umpire: a penalty corner should be awarded to the opposition.
- When a penalty corner is awarded, two of the defending team must go to the shooting circle at the opposite end of the pitch.
- When a penalty stroke is awarded, all non-involved players must go to the other side of the centre-line.

Quicksticks (four-a-side game)

Quicksticks is a game developed by England Hockey for use in primary schools.

The Pitch

The field of play is rectangular. The minimum pitch dimension guideline is that of a standard netball court (30.5m × 15.25m/100 × 50ft) and the maximum pitch dimension guideline is a quarter of a full size hockey pitch (55m × 22.90m/110 × 60yd). There are areas called 'attacking circles' that are equivalent to netball court shooting circles (radius 4.9m).

Goals

Each goal is 2.4m (8ft) wide and 60cm (2ft) high. Each goal is positioned against the outer edge of the backline and firmly secured.

The Rules of Play

There are no goalkeepers in Quicksticks. A team comprises six players of which four are outfield players and two are officials (one manager coach and one umpire). Players rotate every ten minutes.

Duration
Quicksticks is a game of three ten-minute periods with a changeover interval of two minutes between each session. The team

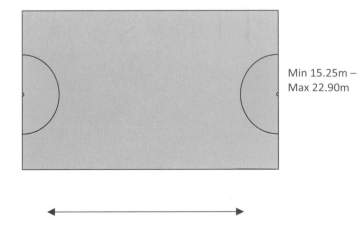

Radius 4.9m

Min 15.25m – Max 22.90m

Min 30.5m – Max 55m

A quicksticks pitch.

A Samba quicksticks hockey goal for children. (photograph supplied by England Hockey, source unknown)

scoring the most goals is the winner. If no goals are scored or the score is equal it will be a draw.

The Ball

The Quicksticks ball is durable and safe for playground use. A variety of balls can be used to differentiate and set learning objectives suitable to the needs of the group.

Scoring a Goal

A penalty goal will be given if a player deliberately stops a ball from crossing the goal-line with their feet or body. All other rules the same as field and mini-hockey.

Player's Clothing and Equipment

Even though the Quicksticks ball is light and soft, players should still wear shin protectors and mouth guards.

Barry Middleton showing great ball carry position with head up to enhance vision. GB v Pakistan 12 June 2008, Setanta Trophy, Dublin, Ireland. (Photograph supplied by England Hockey, © Adrian Kerry)

CHAPTER 3

GETTING STARTED: CLOTHING, EQUIPMENT AND FOOTWEAR

To be able to start playing hockey all you need is suitable clothing with which to attend a club session, which you probably already have. The only extra equipment you would need is a stick, and most clubs will provide you with a stick if you want to try out the sport. Obviously there are other pieces of specialist clothing and equipment but these should only be purchased once you have decided to attend a series of practice sessions and join a club.

Equipment

The Ball

Originally a cricket ball – with a cork centre, string wound and covered with leather – was used for the game. Hockey balls today are usually constructed of a composite core with a PVC outer or a PVC cover depending on the 'feel' that is desired. The ball is about 23cm (9in) in circumference and weighs about 150g (5½oz).

For game play, the balls are dimpled: they have dimples (indentations) similar to those on a golf ball. However, this is not necessarily true of practice balls, which often differ from game balls in quality, feel and texture. When hit correctly this small, hard ball can travel at high speed, which can make the sport dangerous for goalkeepers and players alike, especially since players wear no protection beyond shin, hand and mouth guards.

The Stick

Hockey sticks are usually about 1 metre (36–38in) long and weigh 340–790g (12–28oz). The stick's striking surface is flat on the left side only and is curved on the back side. The ball can only be hit with the flat side (front) side of the stick. It is obvious when looking at the old 'English head' stick that sticks have changed greatly over the years just as the playing surface has changed from grass to an artificial turf pitch. Aside from the various weight/balance characteristics of a stick, the two main features that come into play as far as stick design is concerned are the reinforcement of the stick and the shape of the head of the stick.

Reinforcement of the Stick

All hockey sticks (with the exception of composite and aluminium sticks) begin life as a plain piece of wood. Various materials can then be added to the bare stick to determine its strength and performance characteristics. It follows that the more reinforcement a stick has, the stronger and stiffer the stick, and the harder it will hit the ball (however, it will be less forgiving on a cold day). The main materials that can be added are:

- fibreglass: for basic strength and durability
- kevlar: for increased strength and basic shock absorbency
- carbon: for extra stiffness
- Dyneema: for supreme shock absorbency.

Shape of the Stick Head

There are three main stick head shapes: the Shorti, the Midi and the Hook. The Shorti is the traditional one-piece head,

The sticks have changed over the years, particularly the curve of the stick head.

A wide variety of sticks.

protection as they are made to cover not only the shins but also many of them offer ankle protection too. Some shin pads are constructed from the same foam compound that goalkeeper's pads are made from and are therefore light but durable. Other shin pads are made of canvas and some have a hard plastic cover that is very protective.

Gloves: Hand Protectors

As the game has become quicker and faster, with defenders trying to cover as much of the field as possible and using a horizontal stick, the glove has become a more and more popular piece of protective equipment. At first players would use a cricket batting glove but manufacturers are now producing hockey gloves that are more lightweight with modern foam construction. Whether to use hand protection is a matter of personal choice: some players choose to wear gloves on both hands. The majority of players will wear a glove on the left (top) hand, as this is the one that is likely to get hit when they are putting their stick on the floor.

whereas the Midi and Hook heads are made of several thicknesses of wood glued together (laminated). These different shapes determine both the performance and durability of the head.

A traditional Shorti head is favoured for its better striking capability, which is because its 'sweet spot' is more centred than on other types of head. Shorti heads are also stronger and more durable because they are made of one piece of wood. Laminated Midi and Hook heads are designed to aid ball carry skills, reverse stick play and flicking or delivering aerial balls. They are neither as strong nor as durable as Shorti heads because they are made of several pieces of wood laminated together. However, these differences can be overcome with good care.

Sticks come not only with different shaped heads, but also with different shaped shafts. You will see very few non-straight shafts, but they do exist:

kinked shafts are used by both players and goalkeepers but are not common. For goalkeepers, the kinked-shaft stick offers more of a save area, and for players the sticks can help with control and offer more of a stopping area.

Player Equipment

Besides the goalkeeper, the rest of the playing squad wear very little extra equipment to protect them from the opposition's sticks and balls. However, there are some highly recommended pieces of personal equipment.

Shin Pads

Modern shin pads offer good protection; soccer shin pads will suffice to start with, but hockey shin pads offer much better

Mouth Guards

Because the ball can travel at up to a 160km/h (100mph) and can be deflected up into the air just as quickly, players should be encouraged to wear a gum shields. Whilst the 'do-it-yourself' variety is better than none, it is recommended that players have a fitted gum shield, particularly after they have lost their milk teeth.

Player Clothing and Footwear

Each team will wear a uniform colour. Men's and boys' teams will wear shorts and women's teams will wear skirts. The team kit will include shirts, socks and skirt or shorts of the same colour. Any undergarments (skins) should be the same colour as the shirts. Often clubs will loan

Player equipment: shin pads, gloves, mouth guards, Astroturf shoes.

the team shirts but you will be encouraged to buy your own once you have committed yourself to the team.

Faceguards

At penalty corners, the defenders who have to stand on the line protecting the goal are now starting to wear face masks as there have been some injuries for the post player. They only wear them for the time of the penalty corner and leave them by the goal when the penalty corner is over.

Footwear

To start with, a pair of training shoes will be adequate but as you commit yourself to the game you will need a pair of training shoes known as Astroturf shoes. There are many different types on the market and it is important that your shoes offer some protection for the toes and feet from the hockey ball. Also, because hockey is a game of multi-directional speed changes, it is important that the shoes offer some stability, especially around the ankles.

Goalkeeper Equipment

The equipment you need for goalkeeping will depend on your level and quality of play. However, most of the equipment is used for Under-16 and above, right through to international level.

Goalkeeping Pads

Most goalkeepers will wear foam pads. These are constructed of high-tech foams and various types of laminates, which make the pads exceptionally lightweight while still offering a very high degree of protection and shock absorbency. The pads are so lightweight that they could be blown about by a strong wind. One factor that goalkeepers will need to control is the amount of rebound that these pads offer the ball (see Chapter 11).

Kickers

The main type of kicker in today's game are constructed from the same type of foam as the pads. These kickers offer superior protection to anything previously worn in both size of area covered and in shock absorbency. This shock absorbency is crucial, for if the ball is travelling at high speed and there is little shock absorbency, it will hurt; this in turn will make the goalkeeper hesitant to go for the ball.

Hand Protectors

A number of shots in the game are in the air and as a result the goalkeepers also need to protect their upper body, head and hands. On the hands, they have progressed from wearing gloves to large foam hand protectors because goalkeepers are not allowed to catch the ball, they can only deflect it. The foam used is very similar to that in the pads and kickers, offering lightness and protection. The left hand is a solid flat square of foam whilst the right hand is shaped so that the goalkeeper can hold the stick.

Helmets

We have come a long way since the face masks of the 1980s and now the majority of goalkeepers are looking to ice hockey for head protection. The modern helmet includes neck protection, but the old helmets have to be worn with a neck protector. The helmet unlike the face mask also protects the back of the head.

Shorts

Because the pads only come just above the knee, most goalkeepers will wear padded shorts similar to those worn by ice hockey goalkeepers. Shorts come in different styles but each manufacturer will offer lightweight foam protection on key areas, the thighs and any boned area. They will also offer protection to the lower back area and the kidneys. As some of the varieties of shorts are wrapped around the lower body, and fastened with Velcro, the goalkeeper will wear their own shorts over the top. The key factors in choosing protective shorts are movement and protection.

Body Protection

Other items that the goalkeeper will wear include pelvic protection. These will differ according to the sex of the player: men will wear the equivalent of a cricket 'box'

Goalkeeper wearing the protective equipment.

and women will wear a pelvic protector. They will also wear a chest pad and arm and shoulder protection. This will be made of foam and offer the same movement capabilities and protection. Some goalkeepers will wear separate elbow pads whilst others will wear an all-in-one version that combines elbow, shoulder and chest protection.

The goalkeeper wears a shirt or smock of a different colour to the rest of the team over the top of the goalkeeping equipment.

CHAPTER 4

PLAYING THE GAME

Hockey is a fast-paced sport that offers a fun and competitive way of keeping your body fit and healthy. There are hundreds of field hockey clubs popping up in the UK every year and these cater for all levels, from hockey beginners through to senior professionals.

There are plenty of clubs out there able to accommodate newcomers to the sport of field hockey and many of these can be found by surfing the internet or contacting the governing bodies for the area in which you live. Useful contact addresses and web contacts are at the end of the book. The heart of the game in the UK is found within the thriving club structure and there are more than 1,500 clubs in the UK of varying size and competitive level.

Many of these clubs operate smaller versions of hockey such as mini-hockey for beginners, or indoor hockey to build up players' skills and fitness. Then once you have mastered the basics you can move on to the full scale version of the game by joining a full hockey club.

Hockey considers itself to be a family sport, where barriers such as age, gender and ethnicity bear no importance. This makes hockey an accessible sport, and as such, there are many entry routes to begin playing.

Youngsters Starting Hockey

The best way to get involved in hockey is to make an early start. A player's first step into hockey would be through the Quicksticks game, which is played in primary schools. It is a four-a-side game and introduces the skills of hockey safely. After this the next step would be mini-hockey,

which is a seven-a-side game. Festivals and competitions are run in mini-hockey.

Club–School Links

Often the first introduction to hockey is through a Club–School Link (CSL). CSL occurs when a club is awarded 'ClubsFirst' accreditation from the governing body of hockey in England. The ClubsFirst is a Kitemark, which shows that the club has demonstrated minimum operating standards for dealing with players of the Under-18 age group. At this point a school or a group of schools will join with the club to offer better facilities and coaching. For example, this is a great entry point into club hockey from a school.

The Player Pathway

Traditionally, schools and club hockey will feed players into 'representative honours', which means representation in county, regional and national teams. This starts at district level, with Junior Development Centres (JDCs). There are over 120 planned centres in England, so finding one should not be too difficult and youngsters should be able to ask their teachers for contacts at these centres. Following on from the JDCs are centres known as Junior Academy Centres (JACs). Young people should go to the JAC nearest to where they live, which sometimes may mean that they cross a county boundary. In the past, a young person may have played within their county, which in the case of a large county may have meant a lot of travelling. Hockey is making itself accessible to as many young people as possible, with one of the key aims being that they spend more time on the pitch

than travelling to the pitch. There are approximately forty-two of these centres nationwide.

If a young person is good enough to be selected for a JAC, they may be considered good enough to play for the area of the country where the live, in a Junior Regional Performance Centre (JRPC). There are twelve JRPCs within England, which makes selection to them prestigious. These JRPCs will then play competitive matches in groups of three centres and if you are selected you can play in the Futures Cup. It is from the Futures Cup that the England junior teams are selected.

In Wales there is a similar player pathway; youngsters are identified and placed at an appropriate place on that pathway: Performance Development Centres (PDC), Regional Academies (RA), International Squads and High Performance Centres (HPC).

In Scotland the Performance programme is run in five districts: West, East, Midlands, North and Central. The programme is designed to give young talented players aged 14–18 the opportunity to train regularly alongside other talented players.

All the systems will try and support the player in selection and de-selection, recognizing that some players will mature physically and mentally earlier or later than others. The pathways allow for greater support for all players. Many of our current international players have not been selected at one level or another of junior international teams, and often this helps with the mental toughness of each player to deal with the demands of international hockey.

Once a player reaches eighteen years of age, they are encouraged to attend a National Performance Centre (PDC), which is based a one of Six University consortia:

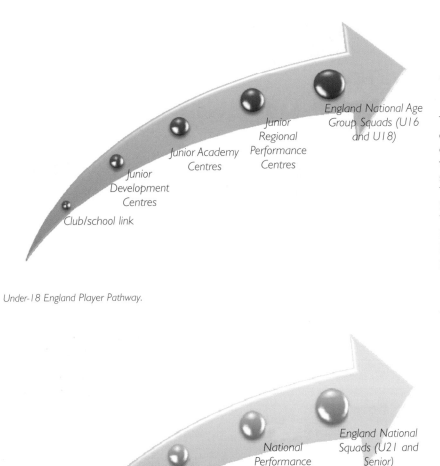

Under-18 England Player Pathway.

Junior Development Centres

Junior Academy Centres

Junior Regional Performance Centres

England National Age Group Squads (U16 and U18)

Club/school link

Over-18 England Player Pathway.

FE or HE link

Senior Clubs

Senior Regional Performance Centres

National Performance Centres

England National Squads (U21 and Senior)

Warwick University, Coventry University, Aston University, Wolverhampton University and Staffordshire University consortium
*   Yorkshire NPC: Sheffield Hallam University, University of Sheffield.

The National Performance Centres are an essential element in providing aspiring players, who want to play at international level, top quality coaching alongside specific strength and conditioning programmes. They will also provide support to athletes in the form of medical and lifestyle advice. The players will continue to play local club hockey and this will enable the sharing of high performance practice throughout the pathway.

Adults Starting Hockey

If you are over eighteen years and have left education the most common way to get involved as a player is to join a club. There are over 1,500 clubs in the UK and over 100 leagues of differing levels. Some clubs are male only, some female only, and some cater for both sexes with some being primarily organized for mixed hockey only.

Clubs play in a variety of leagues, starting with development leagues for youngsters through to the Senior National League. Development leagues are run at local level and are predominantly for young people. The purpose of leagues like these is primarily to offer a competitive opportunity for young people to be able to refine the skills they are learning in training. Various leagues for young people sit above this, and offer appropriate competition.

In England the first place to look for a senior league side is at county level. Each county runs leagues and some counties may run leagues for neighbouring areas depending on the playing population. Teams must work their way up these leagues in order to be promoted to the next stage, which sits at regional level. Regional leagues work in the same way. Once a club has reached the top of their regional league and secured promotion they will then enter the National League.

*   East Midlands NPC: Nottingham Trent University, Nottingham University, Loughborough University consortium
*   Hockey West NPC: University of Bath, University of Bristol, University of the West of England, UWE consortium
*   Manchester NPC: University of Manchester, Manchester Metropolitan University consortium
*   South Coast NPC: Portsmouth University, Southampton University, Solent University consortium
*   West Midlands NPC: University of Birmingham, University of Worcester,

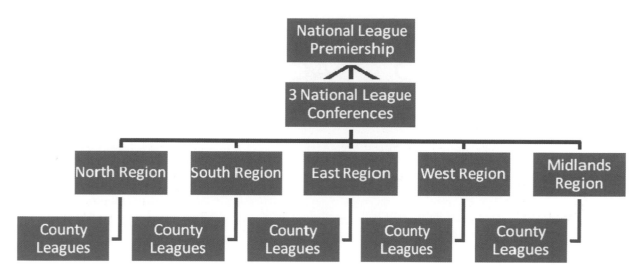

The National League in England.

The winner of the premiership each season secures a place at the European Club Championships, or Euro Hockey league the following season.

Hockey in Europe is becoming much more European, and with the Euro Hockey League comes TV coverage and sponsorship.

Where and When Can I Play?

The heart of hockey lies with the clubs and this will be where lifelong participation takes place. There are plenty of clubs out there able to accommodate newcomers through to performance level players and many of these can be found by surfing the internet or contacting the governing bodies for the area in which you live. Useful contact addresses and web contacts are at the end of the book.

Age	Level of ability	Where	How
School age	Any	School	Schools may offer hockey; if they don't, ask for it! Schools can nominate you to JDC.
School age	Any	Clubs	If your school has a Club–School Link (CSL) ask your PE teacher to give you a club contact. Otherwise, look on the internet for a club that is accredited (ClubsFirst).
College/University	Social	College and University	Many Colleges and Universities offer hockey as a social sport. Contact your Athletic Union for details.
College in conjunction with University	Identified, experienced talented	NPC	England Hockey in the universities have set up six National Performance Centres, which are best equipped to develop your potential.
Over 18 years	Social	Clubs	There are over 1,500 clubs in the UK offering hockey to the community. Contact clubs via the internet: simply search for a contact and off you go. Most clubs run social teams and will welcome you whether you have played before or not.
Over 18 years	Experienced, talented	Clubs	Contact the club via the internet or personal contact if you are at this stage. You have probably come through one of the previous routes.

CHAPTER 5

COACHING AND COACH EDUCATION

The majority of sports focus on the playing of the game and the skills and tactics needed to play the game. It often takes a coach to enable all the players in a team to co-ordinate the use of these skills. A coach may be called a mentor encourager, or a supporter, or have another title, but their work is very important. We only have to look at football and see the impact of people like Ferguson and Scoleri to realise that this is a role of increasing importance.

World class players cannot be produced without the development of world class coaches along the way. There is a structure within England Hockey and its home country partners of Scotland and Wales to produce and develop the UKCC (United Kingdom Coaching Certificates) coaching awards.

The beginning of this framework within England starts with a sports specific Leadership Award. A large amount of contact time within the award is dedicated to coaching. The other aspects of the leadership award are umpiring and officiating, management and administration. These are key factors needed in the organization of hockey. Many young people choose to take part in the Leadership Award as part of the Duke of Edinburgh Award Scheme and this gives them a start within coaching. The award is not specifically for young people; any person of any age can attend a leadership course and gain a useful insight into the world of coaching, umpiring, officiating and managing.

The framework expands at this stage to cover the UK. In 2006, hockey was the first sport to have three levels of coaching endorsed by the UKCC. The coaching awards are also tied to the National Qualifications Framework.

The three levels begin at Level 1. This award provides the essential skills and knowledge necessary to run a safe

England and GB Coach Karen Brown giving instructions to the GB Youth Squad.

and enjoyable session for players to be introduced to the game. The Level 1 award is an assistant coaching award, and Level 1 coaches must operate alongside a coach with a higher qualification who can help them develop their coaching skills. The Level 1 award will give coaches an understanding not only of the principles of coaching, but also an awareness of the safety aspects involved in delivering a session of hockey coaching.

The Level 2 award will give a coach the ability to deliver a full range of techniques and skills in the modern game, and a Level 2 coach may take responsibility for other coaches involved in delivering coaching sessions in a safe and enjoyable way. All Level 2 coaches hold emergency first aid certificates, and have attended a 'safeguarding and protecting young people' course.

The Level 3 award is the qualification for those who wish to coach tactical play and team play to a more advanced level. Ideally all clubs will have at least one Level 3 coach. All details of courses will be on the England Hockey website (*see* Useful Addresses at the end of the book).

Coaching Skills

As with playing, there are a number of core skills that coaches will need to develop: planning, communication, positioning, observation, analysis and feedback.

Planning: Why Do We Need to Plan?

There are a number of issues and questions we need to consider in planning. We need to ask:

*   How many players do we have?
*   What equipment do we need?
*   How much space can we have?
*   Where are we starting from in terms of ability and training?
*   What are our objectives for the session?
*   How can we ensure the players' safety?

After the planning we would then lead the session with the aim of achieving our goals.

The final stage in this process is the review: an evaluation of where we need to revisit our planning and actual play, in order to assess our progress or lack of it.

If you are working with a group of twelve-year-olds who have little or no experience, your planning will be for the following key actions:

*   Learn their names
*   Set the ground rules for the session
*   Make sure it is safe
*   Make sure it is fun
*   Give clear instructions and a demonstration
*   Make sure that you direct the practice at all times
*   Set targets and challenges for your players and yourself
*   Make sure you motivate, praise and encourage
*   Check for understanding by using questions
*   The activity should have variety and not too long should be spent on any one activity
*   Give coaching points one at a time: keep it simple.

Communication

In order to be an effective communicator you first have to be aware that people take in information in different ways, and they also learn in different ways. Some people prefer auditory information, some prefer visual information while others prefer kinaesthetic information. So bearing this in mind, how do we deliver a coaching session?

First, when we speak we give clear, simple information. This would obviously suit the auditory learners who want to listen to information before acting on it.

Second, we would give a demonstration with information back-up, identifying the key points as we go. This will suit those who like visual information.

TOP TIP

Visual learners prefer to learn by seeing
Auditory learners prefer to learn through listening and reading
Kinaesthetic learners prefer to learn through hands-on physical activity

---

The Coaching Process: Plan–Do–Review.

Finally, we would allow the players to practise and try it out: this would help the kinaesthetic learners.

Positioning

Where we stand in relation to our coaching environment and the coaching group is crucial to assisting the communication and coaching relationships. For example, if the sun is shining, the coach should stand facing the sun. If players are squinting into the sun, they will not be able to concentrate on the information being given out. This is especially important for any hearing-impaired youngsters, who will need to be able to see your lips so that they can lip-read.

As a coach you can position the players in a number of ways to enhance the learning environment.

- A **Straight line** enables you to see all the players, depending on the total number of players you have.

- A **Curved line** helps you see all players and helps the players see a demonstration more closely.
- A **V shape** helps you see all players and helps the players see a demonstration.
- A **Circle** is useful when the coach knows the group very well and when they just want to give information, a team talk, and so on.

Observation

The key to good coaching is to be able to see what the players are doing. In order to get a good assessment of a player's performance it is important that the coach looks at the performance from as many

> **KEY POINT**
>
> Make sure you look at a player's performance from as many viewpoints as possible.

different directions as possible. It is a good idea to watch the performance from a minimum of a front view and a side-on view.

Analysis

Try to form your analysis of a player's performance of a skill by working logically through a checklist, such as:

- Position of head
- Body position
- Arm position
- Position of ball in relation to the feet.

It helps to have a picture in your mind about what you are expecting. Until you have plenty of experience it would be useful to carry some actual photos of the skill being performed to show players what it looks like from key coaching points. Be aware that minor deviations would be seen in all of the players but key principles are applied to all players.

A circle positioning is effective with a squad of players that are well known to the coach.

Feedback

Once you have observed and analysed the skill in a player, and compared the performance against a technically good model, you will need to think about how, and what, you will feed back to the player in question.

Remember that when you are coaching you should give one coaching point at a time; this is the same process as giving feedback. The skill comes in identifying which coaching correction point you will feed back first. Once you are happy that the player has worked on this first point you can then feed in another point.

The way that you give feedback is just as important as what you say; whatever you want to feed back you must do it in a positive manner. When working with youngsters, praise and encouragement must be used alongside correction.

Other Coaching Opportunities

Coaching Workshops

England Hockey also organize coaching workshops that take place throughout the year. One of the more popular courses is a Core Skills Workshop. This has been developed by the England Hockey Performance Department. The aim of this workshop is to make sure that those working with young players are given key technical knowledge to place the foundation building blocks in place.

The main areas of delivery are:

* The ball carry position
* V drags
* Hitting
* Pushing
* Passing
* Posting up
* Getting ahead.

Goalkeeping Workshop

The England Hockey Performance Department also provides special workshops on goalkeeping. With this being a specialist area it is important that the key technical points are disseminated.

Other workshops are arranged around major tournaments and events. Full details of coach education course, Level 1, Level 2, Level 3 and coaching workshops can be obtained from England Hockey via the website www.englandhockey.co.uk.

Jonty Clarke slips the ball left for oncoming shot at goal. GB v Mexico 1 March 2008, Olympic Qualifiers, Chile. (Photograph supplied by England Hockey, source unknown)

PART 2

SKILLS AND TECHNIQUES

CHAPTER 6

MOVING WITH THE BALL: BALL CARRY

In hockey 'carrying the ball' means keeping the ball in contact with the stick and moving it around the pitch.

Open Stick Dribble

To dribble is to move with the ball in contact with the stick around the pitch. Doing this with and 'open stick' means the ball is positioned on the right side of the body with the stick. A research project was carried out some years ago that measured the length of time that players had contact with the ball in the game; it amounted to only two minutes. Players should therefore make sure that they are carrying the ball in a strong, effective position to make the best use of the ball contact they have. By using the open stick dribble the player can achieve this, keeping contact with the ball in a strong position, making sure they have as much contact as possible without easily losing possession.

Ball Carry

How Should a Player Carry the Ball?

As a starting point a player should carry the ball ahead of them and to the right (at the 1 or 2 o'clock position). Doing so promotes all the following:

- playing on the forehand
- remaining strong on the ball
- carrying the ball with eyes up to allow for good vision
- being in a position from which you could pass
- being able to move with the ball at a fair pace.

In order to move with the ball while retaining that vitally important peripheral or all-round vision the player should keep their trunk as upright as possible, bending at the knees and not in the back.

Pointing at Pressure

Irrespective of where the player is located on the pitch, the most important element to carrying the ball is that the player is prepared to 'point at pressure', that is, not turn their back on the game in order to protect the ball. In pointing at pressure, the player will give themselves the greatest amount of vision, which will in turn advise them on what pass or dribble options are available, and also what pressure is being placed on them.

> **TOP TIP**
>
> Make sure that you are dribbling the ball towards the space around the defending player to enable you to eliminate the defender on the outside or inside, with a pass or dribble. Too often we protect the ball from an opponent using our body.

Arm Positions in Ball Carry

The left hand and elbow are also huge considerations when thinking about ball carry. There is a natural tendency for a player to carry the ball with left hand and elbow tucked in to their side/hip. If a player can carry the ball with a high left elbow and hand out in front then they will be in a position to make a pass at any moment and without giving opponents too many clues to as to their intentions. Also,

getting the left hand in front will take the ball further away from the carrier's feet, which will allow more vision. Finally, ball manipulation will be made easier (especially on sticky pitches) as contact with the ball when using the reverse can be made beneath the centre of the ball, thus reducing friction that would be created from any downward pressure on the ball.

Pitch Position and Ball Carry

The area on the pitch that a player is located will have a very big bearing on where the ball is to be carried. If on the left-hand side of the pitch, then the most likely passing options will be left to right and as a result the ball will be carried further back in the stance (around 3 o'clock). This will open up the pitch (through the player being prepared to point at pressure) and allow passing and dribble lanes to be opened up both in front of and behind square ('square' means to the left and right of the player and parallel with the endlines). The further forwards the ball is in the left-sided player's stance, the more they restrict their ability to pass square or behind square.

If a player is on the right-hand side, the opposite will be true with more passing options being available right to left. In this scenario the ball carry position is likely to be more directly in front, at 12 or even 11 o'clock. This would be particularly true of a winger looking to deliver a cross (a pass usually made from the edge of the pitch into the centre, often the shooting area). It is also the case for a right half as this would result in an increased range of passing options. The right half is a player that plays behind the forwards and in front of the defenders and supports in attack and defence.

Ball carry position: sideways view.

Ball carry position: front view.

Left wing ball carry position.

Right wing ball carry position.

On the right-hand side it is not uncommon that a player progresses up the pitch in a crab-like manner when not looking to travel as quickly as possible. By leading with the right shoulder, and often moving the ball forward with the reverse stick, the player will truly be able to point at pressure and open many more passing and dribble lanes.

Space and Ball Carry

Another consideration for the player in possession of the ball will be the situation in which they find themselves: this will also dictate how the ball is carried. If a player is in space and wants to move quickly then the right hand can be higher up the stick and there is no need for the stick to be continually in contact with the ball. This more upright position, paying slightly less attention to the ball, will allow the player to move more quickly as they can adopt a more natural running posture. If the player finds themselves in a tight area, under a great deal of pressure, they will first look to secure and/or retain possession as opposed to moving at any great pace. The right hand will drop down the stick to provide greater strength and close control, but the ability to move at speed will be reduced as a result.

The message here is to keep it simple; if the ball does not need to move from a safe and comfortable position in front of you, don't complicate the movement by unnecessary stick and ball contacts.

A key ball carry skill is to move creating angles against opposition; by changing the

KEY PROBLEMS

- Lack of vision: ball too close to feet, right hand too far down the stick
- Lack of strength: right hand too high on the stick
- Lack of control: the angle of the stick head is wrong; move the left hand further away from your body

angle as you pick up the ball you will create new passing options and ball carry lines. The defender will have continually to reassess and realign their defending position.

The ability to move with the ball with strength and confidence is a critical part of the game; each dribbling technique serves a purpose and you must develop each of them to give you options in the game. Luciana Aymar of Argentina is one of the best carriers of the ball in the modern game.

Indian Dribble

The Indian dribble was first seen at the 1956 Olympics. It was named after the superb dribbling skills of the Indian team.

You can use the Indian dribble to change the direction of the ball to beat an opponent, and it is particularly difficult to defend against. The technique is more complicated than the straight dribble. The Indian dribble allows you change direction by moving the ball from left to right and right to left as required.

Your left hand remains at the top of the stick and stays tight on the stick. The right hand is looser and allows the stick to rotate within it.

This is one of the main areas of error for young people who grasp tightly with the right hand, and as a result they cannot turn the stick quickly. Your left hand should do most of the work with your right hand helping to fine-tune and support the left.

The ball should be out in front of the body and moved in a zigzag pattern across the ground. Try to keep the ball out as far as possible, as it is easier to manoeuvre the stick that way and you will not get the top of your stick into your body.

As you move down the pitch try to transfer your body weight from left foot to right foot and vice versa. When you see the defender commit to one way, try and attack the other side at a fast pace.

One-handed Dribble

Whilst stressing that the two-handed dribble is the style that should be encouraged,

it is necessary to discuss the one-handed dribble as it has a place in the playing of the game. With a one-handed dribble you can carry the ball wide on the left and the right away from your opponent. Ideally you should try and keep it far enough away from your opponent that they will not be able to reach it. You should try and maintain your vision and only use this technique when absolutely necessary as it is a weak position in which to carry the ball.

For a left-hand reverse stick dribble, try and carry the ball in the 11 o'clock or 12 o'clock position if moving to the right. As soon as you have space, transfer the ball across and get into a two-handed dribble as soon as possible.

For a right-hand open stick dribble, the ball should be carried at 1 o'clock but you should have moved your right hand to the top of the stick and taken the left hand off the stick. Again, as soon as you have space, transfer your right hand down the stick and get your left hand back at the top of the stick.

In order to be able to carry the ball with effect in the game, it is necessary for the players to develop their footwork and agility. What follows is a number of drills to help you develop ability to move with the ball.

Basic Footwork Drills (for First Timers and Junior Players)

First Set-up

Set out two lines of nine cones (tall cones if possible) spaced evenly over 80m (25yd). Place a normal small cone on the fourth cone each side.

Basic Footwork
Players slalom through the cones as quickly as possible.

Coaching Points
- Turn on the balls of the feet. This increases ability to push off quicker,

Indian dribble showing a poor position: the bottom hand is too tight and restricts movement.

Indian dribble showing good body, hand and head position.

Reverse stick one-handed ball carry position.

Open stick one-handed ball carry position.

prevents ankle injuries, and minimizes falling over.
• Use the arms to generate speed.

Change of Pace: Acceleration

Players run at 50 to 60 per cent of full pace to the small cone, and then accelerate at full pace to the end of the slalom.

In order to keep the practice progressive and monitor progress, coaches could introduce races, which might be knockout races, team races or individual races. It can be useful to time players, and to monitor their increase in speed over weeks, but also to monitor their technique. Coaches can also use this exercise to analyse the difference in a player's ability to move fast with and without the ball. If there is a problem, is it that they are physically slow (without the ball they are slow, but not much difference with the ball) or not technically correct at ball carrying (quick players whose times are significantly slower with the ball)?

Second Set-up

Take the fifth and sixth cone from the slaloms, and place between the seventh and eighth, and eighth and ninth cones on both lines. There are now four pairs of widely-spaced cones, and five pairs of more closely spaced cones.

Change of pace: Deceleration

Players slalom through the cones as fast as possible. The spacing of the cones dictates the speed at which they can run.

Coaching Points
• Use your vision to see what pace is required at each section.
• Take smaller steps to decelerate.

Again, in order to keep the practice progressive and monitor progress, coaches could introduce races of different kinds, time players, and monitor their increase in speed over weeks, and also technique.

Third Set-up

Return the cones to their original places. Place small cones on even-numbered cones on one side, and on odd ones on the other. These cones make it easier for players to determine which slalom is theirs.

Change of Direction: Acceleration and Deceleration

Players have to run from side to side, touching the tip of each cone of their slalom. This encourages changing pace up and down, as well as side to side movement. Once the player from the opposite queue has touched their second cone the other line starts.

Coaching Points
• Both feet need to be in contact with the ground ('planted') when turning.
• The outer foot is used to brake and push off, and should be outside of the centre of gravity. For example, if you are turning to the left the right foot is your outer foot and if turning to the right your left foot becomes the outer foot.
• The inner foot is used to take weight off the outer foot and add extra grip and control.
• Players are not to side-step from side to side, but to run with feet facing forward, and then turn them at the cone.

Basic Ball Carrying (for First Timers and Junior Players)

First Set-up

Space out two lines of nine cones (tall cones if possible) evenly over 80m (25yd). Place a normal small cone on the fourth cone each side.

Basic Ball Carrying

Players slalom through the cones as fast as possible.

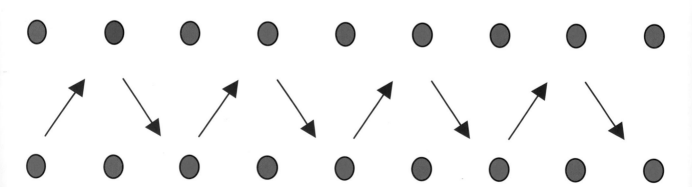

Basic cone set-up for the drills on ball carry and footwork.

Coaching Points

- Carry the ball as much as 95 per cent of the slalom on the open stick. This means keeping the ball on your right-hand side.
- Use the feet to change direction.
- 'Glide' through the cones.
- Keep the stick on the ball, with smooth dribbling and eliminate 'tip-tapping' as it shows loss of control. To eliminate 'tip-tapping', keep continuous contact with the ball so there is no sound of stick on the ball. (Tip-tapping refers to the sound of the stick on the ball. It is a lazy way of dribbling where the ball carrier takes their stick off the ball and has to keep reconnecting with the ball making a tapping noise each time the stick touches the ball.)

Change of Pace: Acceleration

Players run at 50 to 60 per cent of full pace to the small cone, and then accelerate at full pace to the end of the slalom.

To keep the practice progressive and monitor progress, coaches can introduce races: knockout races, team races or individual races. Coaches can also time players, which is useful in order to monitor any increase in speed over weeks. Coaches should also note any improvement in technique.

Coaches can also use this exercise to analyse the difference in a player's ability to move fast with and without the ball. If there is a problem, is it that they are physically slow (without the ball they are slow, but not much difference with the ball) or not technically correct at ball carrying (quick players whose times are significantly slower with the ball)?

Second Set-up

Take the fifth and sixth cone from the slaloms and place them between the seventh and eighth, and eighth and ninth cones on both lines.

Change of Pace: Deceleration

Players slalom through the cones as quickly as possible. The spacing of the cones dictates the speed at which they run.

This is exactly the same as the basic footwork drill except that players are carrying the ball. The ball-carrying principles are also the same as when you are moving without being in contact with the ball.

In order to keep the practice progressive and monitor progress, coaches can again introduce races of different kinds. The timing of players is useful to monitor increase in speed over weeks, but also to monitor technique.

Coaches can also use this exercise to analyse the difference in a player's ability to move fast with and without the ball. If there is a problem, is it that they are physically slow (without the ball they are slow, but not much difference with the ball) or not technically correct at ball carrying (quick players whose times are significantly slower with the ball)?

Third Set-up

Return the cones to their original places. Place small cones on even-numbered tall cones on one side, and on odd-numbered cones on the other. These cones make it easier for players to determine which slalom is theirs.

Ball Carrying: Open Stick Only

Change of Direction: Acceleration and Deceleration

Players have to dribble their ball around their big slalom. The footwork is the same as in the footwork drill, except they now have a stick and ball and must go around the outside of the cones. All the ball-carrying principles apply. Sticking out the left elbow assists turning from left to right. Remember, 'glide' with the ball.

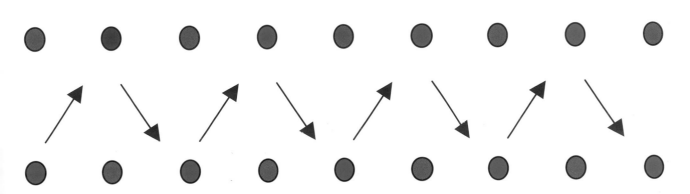

Basic cone set-up for the drills on acceleration and deceleration.

Advanced Ball Carrying (for Players Experienced in the Drills)

Setting the cones out evenly, even when they are close together, does not teach improvisation. Players fall into a rhythm, and while this is necessary when teaching the basics in order to achieve the required repetition, it is not good for long-term athlete development (LTAD).

To make the sessions more advanced, the cones are placed randomly in terms of distance apart and the line that they are on. The players have to have good vision, and the ability to adapt constantly and accelerate and decelerate accordingly as well as to change direction.

For Junior Players, Low-Level Ability Players

Set-up

Space out evenly two lines of nine cones (tall cones if possible) over 80m (25yd).

Place a normal small cone on the fourth cone on each side. Players must make a pass to a teammate between every cone from start to finish.

Coaching Points

- Those on the left-hand side of the cones, make sure that you keep the ball outside the right foot.
- Those on the right-hand side, make sure the ball comes across the body so that it is outside the right foot.
- Keep the stick and the ball together, from first touch to pass.
- Feet to face forwards.
- Glide.

Ball carry position to enable the pass.

CHAPTER 7

MOVING THE BALL

The ability to move the ball and pass the ball is crucial to the game of hockey. There are a variety of passes that can be used and each of them offers a combination of power, subtlety and variation. One of the keys to good play is to know when and where to use these passes. The passes should be practised when stationary and on the move. In fact, on the move is often where they are most effective.

To be an effective passer means you will become a better team player in all areas of the game: forward, midfield and defence.

The ability to collect the ball also enhances the play. Your first touch is crucial. With a good first touch you can gain a metre of space, beat a player, make a pass, or set up to make an accurate and strong pass or shot.

Similarly, with a good pass you can make space for the receiving player, move the defence out of position, cut the defence apart or simply build an attack.

Defining a Good Pass

A good pass is one that enables the receiving player to do something productive with their first touch. The receiving player should not have to control a bobbling ball, stretch for the ball or alter their run because the pass is too early or delayed, or have to move towards the ball for an underhit pass.

A pass should be:

- accurate
- correctly paced
- well timed.

These aspects of passing should be built into all your practice sessions, whether through simple drill by purely concentrating on unopposed and therefore unpressured passing, or by more advanced conditioned games that require passing against opposition and in an environment with both time and space restricted.

Key Coaching Points

- Use simple passing drills to warm up.
- Encourage players to keep it simple and clearly show where they want to receive the pass.
- Try to get your players and team-mates to anticipate the next move so as to place the ball in front of where the player is moving.

Before a player receives a pass they should have some idea of exactly what their options will be after receipt of the ball. They need to get into the habit of pre-scanning before receiving the ball and then scanning to check that the options are still available. The options will normally involve what

Receiving the ball, with a balanced and strong body position, the low bottom hand as upright as possible.

The hit: preparation.

The hit: execution.

The hit: follow-through.

space is available to move into, what space they may be able to pass the ball through and move the ball into.

Key Receiving Tips

- Know what you want to do with the ball before the pass is made by pre-scanning and checking the options available.
- Move away from the space you start in and want to receive the ball in to create a space to use.
- Move towards the ball: do not wait for it to come to you.
- Re-check the options that were available on the pre-scan to see if they still exist.
- After pre-scanning and identifying where the opposition and the spaces are, choose the next best option to use for the best of your team. This means that your team keep possession or eliminate one or more of the opposition and ultimately that your team may score a goal.
- Keep your feet moving and move your body into the best position for you to maintain possession of the ball.

We will now look at the variety of passes that can be used. You should try to make sure that you can use all of them to enhance your game. Some common passing techniques are the hit, the push, the slap or sweep pass, the reverse pass, the first time or wall pass and the aerial pass.

The Hit

The hit seems to be a dying skill on the new artificial turf pitches as most people do not fully appreciate the strengths and advantages of using it as a tool for success. Hitting the ball gives greater power over a longer distance. It can help change the point of attack for your team and out-manoeuvre the opposition. You should be able to hit off either foot – left or right – but in general it will be with your left foot forward. By transferring

the weight from your back foot (right) to your front foot (left) you should get maximum power. In a tight situation you should be able to use a clip hit. With a clip hit the swing will be quicker as you lower your top hand (left) down to meet your bottom hand (right). In essence, this makes the stick a shorter lever that provides a quicker swing. The key factor is to make sure that the hands work together on the stick and not separately, working against each other.

Key Coaching Points

- Try to maintain a sideways position with your left shoulder pointing towards the target.
- Make sure your body is in a strong position; bend your knees and lower your centre of gravity.
- Try to make sure that as you hit the ball it is level with your left foot.
- Make sure your hands are together on the stick so that you can make them work together.
- Look at the back of the ball all the way through the action. This means you will keep your head down.
- Follow through towards the target by transferring your weight through the ball in the direction of where you want the ball to go.

When To Use a Clip Hit

You would use a clip hit when the opposition are close by. By lifting the stick you may lose possession of the ball. The longer the stick takes to swing, the longer the opposition have to steal the ball. Once you become competent with the hit, try to add some deception to its placement by altering the wrist position at the point of impact. Delayed hands will help you hit to the right with deception.

To use a reverse hit you must reverse most of the actions from an open side hit. It is like playing a backhand in racket sports but you must make sure that you hit the ball with the flat side of the stick.

The Push Pass

The push pass is a method of moving the ball around the pitch and to team members. It is used for passes over a short distance and should be easily executed whilst moving with the ball, particularly if the ball carry position is good. For a good ball carry position to be achieved the ball is carried on the right-hand side of the body and slightly out in front. It is a good pass to use in a tight situation as the stick does not leave the ball until the pass has been executed. This makes it difficult for the opposition to steal the ball from you.

Because there is no backswing involved, the push pass is quickly executed in a tight area. Also, it offers a high amount of deception that the opposition will find difficult to read. The keys to delivering a good push pass are quick footwork, and ideally your body being in a strong delivery position, which will be determined by the amount of time you have. In a situation where you have plenty of time, quick footwork will get your body lined up correctly: left foot forward, pointing in the direction of the pass.

The strongest passing position is left foot forward, a sideways position so the right foot is behind. The weight is transferred from the back foot (right) through the pass onto the front foot (left). This should give good contact of the stick on the ball and whilst power is not crucial, it always helps.

Key Coaching Points: Push Pass

- Grip: the left hand is at the top of the stick, the right hand further down the stick for control.
- The stick starts in contact with ball and only leaves contact once the pass has been executed.
- No backswing is used.
- Adopt a low posture and follow through to the target.
- Transfer weight from the back foot (right) through to the front foot (left).
- Use quick footwork throughout.

The push: preparation.

The push: execution.

The push: follow-through.

The Slap or Sweep Pass

This is a passing skill that has been introduced in the modern game because of the surface that the game is played on. Unfortunately this stroke has been used at the expense of the previous two skills and has generated a great deal of predictability in the game, which develops mediocrity.

The slap should be played in a shooting situation and where more power is required but where there is no time to get into a hitting position.

The slap or sweep can be played with hands apart or hands together, although to put deception on the pass it is probably better to have your hands together on the stick. The body position would be the same as for a hit or push, which is sideways. The stick is then taken back along the ground in a large circular action. The ball is often slightly further away from the feet. In the attacking circle you can angle your stick slightly backwards at the point of contact, thus enabling the ball to

Slap or sweep: preparation, stick stays on the floor throughout the action.

Slap or sweep: follow-through towards the target.

The reverse stick push pass, ball out in front, right hand controls the stick.

The Reverse Stick Push Pass

This pass has mainly been used over a very short distance, but recently teams are starting to utilize the push pass, or 'reverse stick hit', particularly away from deep defence and crossing the ball in to the circle for shots on target.

It has been thought that a reverse stick pass had a low success rate, but teams have shown that this is no longer the case; therefore, it should be practised for an equal amount of time as the open stick variations.

With a reverse stick pass the right foot would tend to be forwards but all other coaching points would be the same as the open stick passes.

First Time or Wall Pass

This is a pass that is very effective but rarely practised, as it requires your teammates to recognize the space to be exploited and move into it. Whilst pre-scanning, if you identify a big space into which you can move the ball, allow the ball to move first time off your stick into that space.

The expertise of the passer in this skill is to angle the stick so that it will rebound into the space for a teammate to pick up in flow. It is also useful if you recognize that you may not have time to collect the ball without the opposition putting you under pressure.

It must be recognized that there is element of risk in this skill as you are dependent on your teammates being aware of the possibility of the pass and the ball being moved on straight away. However, with the risk comes a match-changing pass if it is successful. Get your teammates to practise this pass so that it becomes successful and effective.

The Aerial Pass

The aerial pass is used a great deal in the men's game but not so much in the women's game. It is usually used by the

lift, but in general play it is important to shift your weight forward so that the ball does not lift.

Key Coaching Points: Sweep or Slap Pass

- The grip is either with hands together at the top of the stick, or hands apart, as in the push pass.
- The stick is moved away from the ball in a large circular action along the ground.
- Players should adopt a low posture and follow through to the target.
- Players should try to develop some deception in this pass, as it is the easiest pass for the opposition to intercept.

Aerial pass preparation: stick stays in contact with the ball, low body position.

defenders to clear the defending area, especially if the opposition are pressing the ball and blocking all the available outlet passes.

It is generally believed that you need good overall body strength for this pass, but in truth it is a technique that all players should learn at an early age. The keys to success are timing and co-ordination, which are crucial.

Again it is a sideways technique and you have the ball further in front of you than you would for the push pass. The angle of the stick is such that the ball will be propelled into the air with a transfer of weight once again from back foot (right) to front foot (left) in the direction of your target.

Key Coaching Points: Aerial Pass

- Adopt a low body position; bend your knees.
- Make sure the ball is in front of your feet.
- Rotate through the hips as you propel the ball.
- Be realistic as you practice about how far you can propel the ball.
- Transfer your weight from your back foot (right) to your front foot (left).

If the ball is too close you will be cramped and will then just try and lift the ball with your arms; it is important to make this a body action and not just an arm action. Once you have mastered this skill you can vary the distance so that teammates can run into open space to collect the aerial pass.

Aerial pass follow-through: head stays still throughout the action.

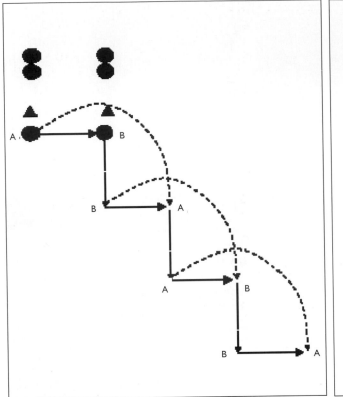

The step pass drill.

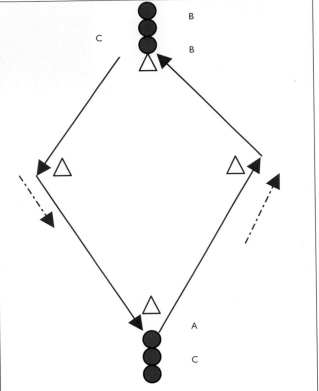

The diamond pass drill.

Practices to Help Develop Your Passing

1 The Step Pass

In pairs, players move forward with the ball.

Player A passes the ball square to Player B. To 'pass the ball square', means the ball is passed parallel to the backline, that is, at right angles to the pitch.

Player A runs round behind B to be available for a pass from B.

Continue and repeat the movement with B supporting A, and so on.

First practice passing right to left.

Then practice passing left to right.

Accelerate on to the ball and finish with a shot.

2 The Diamond Pass

In groups of no less than four, Players A and B move diagonally with the ball towards the cone to their right and pass the ball diagonally left to the next person in line.

After passing, players follow their pass and join the end of opposite queue.

Players C and D receive the ball and repeat the practice.

This practice can be changed with players moving towards the cone to their left.

3 The Three-Man Weave

Players start in a line of three.

Player B passes left to A and follows the line of the pass, running behind A to be available for a pass.

A moves diagonally to receive the ball and then passes to C.

C moves diagonally to receive the ball and pass to B who is supporting.

Try to keep the ball on the open stick. Accelerate on to the ball, and finish with a shot.

In summary, the more you increase your ability to make effective passes to your teammates the more valuable you will become. There are many passing techniques and each have their place in the game.

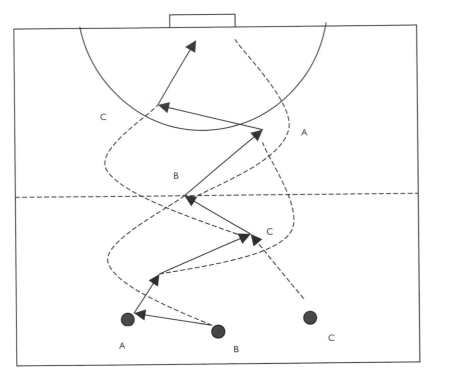

The three-man weave.

Practice will help you improve the technical aspects of playing the game. As you practice you should increase the level of pressure because your ability to make the correct choice of pass under pressure is the key to effective and successful hockey. By increasing your variation of passes you are maximizing your options; this will keep your opponents guessing, giving you greater success and improving your game.

Anne Panter showing excellent ball carry position down the right wing. GB v Ireland, Setanta Trophy 14 June 2008, Dublin, Ireland. (Photograph supplied by England Hockey, © Adrian Kerry)

CHAPTER 8

EVASION SKILLS

Avoiding or evading the opposition on the field has become increasingly difficult. The surface that the game is played on has enabled the defender to cover more area on the pitch and therefore the players have to develop advanced methods of evasion. The main evasion skills are the V drags and 3-D skills. In hockey, defending generally means one of the opposition will try to mark or defend one of your team. But in some cases they may decide to try and cover or defend an area of the pitch and prevent the opposition from moving the ball through that area. Evasion means to eliminate the opposition, and avoid losing the possession of the ball.

Drags and elimination skills allow you to change direction, create new angles of movement and eliminate the opposition players as you move with the ball. The appropriate use of these skills will increase with greater competence on the ball.

Before you can develop your elimination skills you must have a good ball-carrying position, which will give you good vision and control. If your vision and control are good, you can make an appropriate decision about eliminating your opposition. Remember that the second the ball comes off the stick it becomes anybody's ball, so do not send it too far.

The simpler you can make the action the more likely you are to succeed.

You can drag the ball left or right, or lift the ball over a horizontal outstretched stick. Every time you drag the ball you change the line on which you move, with the aim of getting your opponent off balance to eliminate him with the drag or to off-balance him so you can exploit the space the drag has created. Another way to begin an attack is by dispossessing the opposition by using the tackle. More information on tackling skills can be found in Chapter 9.

The V Drags

V Drag Right to Left

This is the technique for moving the ball from your right to your left. The first principle you need to apply is running at an angle towards your opponent's left foot (your right), with the intention of passing them down their left-foot side. You have to make this as convincing as possible to be able to commit the defender and open up the space you want to exploit. This has to be quite exaggerated as the defender will take their cues from your actions and you need to convince them you will do one thing, whilst opening up the opportunity for you to do something quite different. The idea is to use your body and weight transfer to commit the defender. The next stage is vital as you identify the defender's weight shift to cut out your right channel, pull the ball back and across to your left, making a V-shape with the ball. You will need quick feet and quick hands. Try to keep your stick in contact with the ball and make sure you do not get too close before you try and execute this skill.

Key Coaching Points

- Move towards the left foot of your opponent (your right), as though you are going to pass down your right channel.
- Having pre-scanned for your options, and recognizing the space you want to exploit, watch for the defender committing. As they react to your movement right, they may even commit by putting their stick down to block your way right.
- When they have committed it is your time to commit to the drag.

You need to react to the defender's movements and keep assessing your options.
- With your stick in contact with the ball, make your drag back and to the left; try to keep your feet moving at all times.
- Accelerate into the space and away from your opponent.

V Drag Left to Right

The drag right is almost a mirror image of the drag right to left, but the advantage of the drag left to right is that it exploits the non-stick side of the defender, and if executed well should offer you more space to move into and set up an attack.

Key Coaching Points

- Move towards the right foot of your opponent (your left), as though you are going to pass down your left channel.
- Having pre-scanned for your options, and recognizing the space you want to exploit, watch for the defender committing and as they react to your movement left, they may even commit by putting their stick down to block your way left.
- When they have committed it is your time to commit to the drag; you need to react to the defender's movements and keep assessing your options.
- With your stick in contact with the ball, make your drag back and to the right; try to keep your feet moving at all times.
- Accelerate into the space and away from your opponent.

The V Drag. (a) Preparation; (b) execution; (c) completion.

V Drag Practice (see diagram on page 52)

Remember the key ball-carrying position enabling you to see and manoeuvre the ball.

With the V Drag it is possible to keep adding to the skill by introducing a dummy or fake move. On each side you make out that you are about to pass the ball before using a wide drag.

Dummy Drag: Right Drag Left

Key Coaching Points

*   Adopt the basic grip, with the left hand at the top of the stick and right hand at a comfortable distance down the stick, about one-third to half-way down.
*   Pretend ('dummy') to make a reverse stick pass to the right and let the stick go past the ball.

*   Wide drag with the open stick to the left.
*   Control the ball with reverse stick.
*   Scan.
*   Cut out the defender's line of recovery.

Dummy Drag: Left Drag Right

Key Coaching Points

*   Adopt the basic grip.
*   Dummy an open stick pass to the left, let the stick go past the ball.
*   Wide drag with the reverse stick to the right.
*   Control the ball with the open stick.
*   Scan.
*   Cut out the defender's line of recovery.

In the modern era and the advent of the artificial turf pitches the attackers have had to recognize the need for rethinking their evasion skills. The defenders are now

playing with a horizontal stick to block the routes that the attackers want the ball to go in. Quick thinking is essential. If you recognize a space on the field behind a defender who has put themselves into a position where they can be easily beaten – that is, their feet are square to you the ball carrier – you must take advantage of it. The easiest way to do this is by pushing the ball into the space and accelerating on to it before the defender has time to turn and collect the ball. The key factors are not to send it too far into the space that you cannot re-collect it before one of the opposition does.

Push and Run Around

The push and run around is an extension of dribbling, and is usually used by a player going down the wing on either side as there tends to be more space in those areas of the pitch. You need to recognize when a defender has 'squared up' and

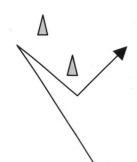

there is space behind them. You can either push the ball through their legs or down either side of them. You must then accelerate on to regain possession of the ball. Remember that the second the ball comes off the stick it becomes anybody's ball, so do not send it too far.

Key Coaching Points

- Adopt the basic grip.
- Fake to go down the open stick side of the defender.
- As the defender's stick comes across, push the ball past the left foot or through the feet and run around and collect it.
- Scan.
- Cut out the defender's line of recovery.

3D Skills or Aerial Skills

The Low Lift

As mentioned above, attackers have to read the situation being created by the defenders and the majority of defenders are covering more of the pitch with the horizontal stick and blocking the pitch pathway of the ball. Because of this factor, the attackers have to develop the use of what is termed 3D skills or aerial skills. As you recognize a defender's stick closing down the land route, you should then manoeuvre the ball into an angle that makes it easy to lift whilst going forward. As a beginner, you may have to pull the ball back towards your own goal before lifting it, but as you develop your skills it is more effective if you can do this on the move going forward.

Key Coaching Points: Low Lift with Open Stick

- Adopt the basic grip.
- Fake to go down the open stick side of the opponent.
- Wide drag with the reverse stick.
- Keep the ball out in front.

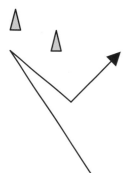

V Drag practice.

- Lift the ball as the flat stick challenge comes in.
- Scan.
- Cut out the defender's line of recovery.

Key Coaching Points: Low Lift with Reverse Stick

- Adopt the basic grip.
- Fake to go down the reverse stick side of the opponent.
- Wide drag with the open stick to the left.
- Keep the ball out in front.
- Lift the ball as the flat stick challenge comes in.
- Scan.

- Cut out the defender's line of recovery.

Evasion skills, and especially the appropriate use of them, are difficult to master. You need to begin by identifying the skill you want to develop and start at walking pace without any pressure of opposition. As you develop the skill, increase the pressure by adding a passive defender who will gradually become more competitive. You can measure your improvement by using a stopwatch: how quickly can you execute the movement whilst keeping control of the ball?

If you are a forward, you must practise evasion skills but as a midfielder and

defender they will also be a key point of your own game.

Keep your opponents guessing by developing as many of the evasion skills as possible. If you only use one method of evasion the opposition will soon work that out and you will find that you are struggling to eliminate any of the opposition players. You will always have your favourite method but by working on the others you will give yourself a greater chance of success.

Low lift with open stick: the ball stays in close contact with the stick.

Low lift with reverse stick: the ball stays in close contact with the stick.

CHAPTER 9

DEFENDING SKILLS

One of the key elements of hockey is for your team to have possession of the ball. There will be times when you need to regain the ball from the opponents' possession. It is vital that your defenders develop an expertise when tackling and trying to gain possession of the ball. But when your team does not have the ball, you are all defenders and so defending is a key core skill that you will need to develop to give you and your team the best chance of success.

This chapter introduces several skills not defined before.

- Tackle is the moment of contact between the defender and the attacker who has possession of the ball, where the defender tries to take the ball off the attacker.
- Intercept is when a defender gains possession of the ball when it is in space between two attackers.
- Clean tackle is taking possession of the ball and being able to effect the next skill.
- Block tackle is where a defender will block the attacker's route by placing the stick horizontal on the pitch.

It is possible to gain possession by positioning yourself and by making interceptions as the opponents try to pass the ball. To intercept the ball, you have to develop your ability to anticipate the movement of the ball thereby helping you to get to the ball first. You also improve your success rate for tackling if you are reading the game and anticipating the opponent's next move, this will usually come through match practice and experience.

The keys to making a good tackle are getting low to the ground and having a good amount of mobility. Don't plant your feet and have patience. Before you need to resort to the tackle it is possible to manipulate the player by your body position to channel them into an area that makes it easier for you to make a clean tackle.

Closing Down and Channelling

The main idea of closing down and channelling is to dictate to the attacker which space they should use. In this way you are not allowing the attacker to determine which space they can use. This action is known as channelling the player with the ball and it will give you control of a difficult situation.

When channelling you should use the lines of the pitch to assist you and in general you should try to push the player with the ball wide to the sidelines or the baseline. If you are in the middle of the pitch you would try and channel them onto your open stick side or the open stick side of one of your teammates, thereby making an opportunity for a block tackle.

Key Coaching Points: Closing down and Channelling, Open Stick

- Close down on a curve to force the attacker onto the open stick side.
- Maintain the distance of a stick and step away from the opponent.
- Get as side-on as possible, thus keeping your mobility.
- Jab with stick and fake with the body to keep opponents eyes on the ball and to prevent them from seeing any passing options.

Generally we want to close down the area and channel onto the open stick where the defence is the strongest. There are, however, circumstances when channelling on the reverse side is required. The first is if the attacker receives on the left of the defender and the defender is not in a position to overtake and force the attacker onto the open stick. The second is when there is no defensive cover in place and to force the attacker into the open stick would lead to greater danger. This would tend to happen in the defensive inside left channel and that is why the general principle is to force the attacker wide to the nearest wing or side of the pitch.

Key Coaching Points: Closing Down and Channelling, Reverse Stick (see photo on page 56)

- Pre-scan to see if cover defender is in place.
- Close down on a curve to force the attacker onto the reverse side.
- Maintain the distance of a stick and a step away from opponents.
- Get as side-on as possible – thus keeping your mobility.
- Fake with the stick and body to keep opponent's eyes on the ball to prevent them from seeing any passing options.

Marking

There are two main ways of marking in hockey: man-to-man marking and zone marking.

Man-to-man marking is where each defender marks one of the opposition. This is very common in most levels of hockey as it is easy for the team to recognize if a member of the opposition is 'free' and not being marked. The defender will then have the choice of front, side and back marking their opponent. It is the defender who decides which will be the most effective in the area of the pitch they are in. Modern hockey will see more front and side marking, with the main aim of intercepting and gaining possession of the ball.

The second form of marking is where a team decides to employ zone marking. This is where an area of the pitch is given to each player and they are responsible for marking anyone who comes into that zone.

The main aim of marking is to prevent your opponent from gaining possession of the ball.

Interception

The defender needs to be in a position that is on the ball side of their opponent and which will enable them to see both their opponent and the ball. The distance from their opponent will be determined by the distance the ball is away from them and the opponent. The closer the ball, the closer the defender must be to their opponent. This will also help the defender to provide cover for teammates while still fulfilling their own marking responsibilities.

Key Coaching Points: Interception, Open Stick

- Adopt the basic grip.
- Beat your opponent to the ball.
- Hold the stick down low, early in the move.
- Receive on the head of the stick so that you can move off with the ball.
- Scan for passing options.

Key Coaching Points: Interception, Reverse Stick

- Adopt the basic grip.
- Beat your opponent to the ball.
- Receive on the hook of the stick.
- Angle the stick forward slightly to control the ball.

Channelling. (a) Use the sideline as another defender; keep the attacker out to the side. (b) Keep your stick low to the ground and do not allow the attacker to cut inside. (c) Force the attacker on to your teammate's stick.

(a)

(b)

(c)

Channelling: here is a good example of closing down reverse stick, forcing the attacker away from the danger zone.

- Get the ball to the open stick side quickly and scan for passing options.

Tackling

When making a tackle in a situation where the play has been slowed down or is in a confined area, you must be able to get low to the ground and get your stick flat on the ground so that you can cover as wide an area as possible. In this way you can protect your feet from being hit and therefore giving a free hit to the opposition. You must also try to maintain mobility at all times: if the attacker does go past you, you need to respond and recover as quickly as possible.

In open play situations the key factor will be to know when to time your tackle. You will need patience as you shadow and move back with your opponent, commonly called 'track back'. Make your move when you are in the best position, or

channel the opponent onto a teammate's stick. If you commit too early you may be easily beaten.

Beginners

To develop a good tackling position you will need to follow the same principles as stated for evasion skills. Identify the skill and walk it through first of all without any opposition. A general principle for youngsters to follow is to match up stick to stick with the opposition; if you line up eyes to eyes you will be more easily beaten on your reverse stick. Take up a side-on position and take a couple of big steps to your left. This should encourage your opponent to run the ball onto your open stick. Keep your stick on the ball at all times and as early as possible to restrict the attacker's passing options.

Keep sideways and keep mobile; a low body position with good footwork should

make you strong enough to withstand the opponent's strength at all times.

The Tackle or Jab Tackle

The first thing you need to do is engage with your opponent and try and slow them down. The easiest way of doing this is by adopting the principles suggested for beginners, above.

Starting Position

- Adopt a side-on position.
- Take two big steps to left of the opponent as they come towards you.
- Keep your stick on or near to the ground.

This starting position gives cues to your opponent that they will not pass you

Jab tackle: here the defender has just released the stick from two hands and is looking to distract the opposition and possibly gain possession of the ball.

easily. As long as possible keep the stick in two hands in front of and protecting your feet.

Executing the tackle

As they get closer, extend the stick towards them and the ball; this should mean that they will look down to protect the ball and this in turn will slow them down. As the ball comes off their stick and is unprotected you need to be ready to jab your stick towards the ball. To get greater extension you should make sure that you go from two hands to one hand and back to two hands as quickly as possible. When teaching this to very young players you could give them the picture of a lizard's tongue, because that is how quickly the move should be made. They should also think of their body position as that of a lion getting ready to pounce. Giving them these images helps them

maintain a good body posture throughout.

As you jab the stick in the direction of the ball your intention may not be to win the ball, but you will stop the momentum of the attacker. If you do jab the ball, one of your teammates may well pick up the loose ball instead.

You can also make a dummy tackle before you are ready to execute the real thing. You should also try and reach out as far away from you as possible, still giving yourself chance to execute the block tackle if needed.

Block Tackle, Open Stick

The block tackle is where a defender will block the attacker's route by placing the stick horizontal on the pitch. The block tackle is used when you are in a good

position and you do not want the attacker to go any further. It is vital that your deep defenders employ this tackle on the edge of the shooting circle to prevent forwards entering the circle and getting shots away. You will need to make sure you are in a good position: ideally low to the ground with your weight forward, left foot in front of right foot.

Ideally you should try and keep both hands on the stick, but if you are reaching forward then there is a chance that you might just use your left hand. You should use little or no backswing and the stick should be held as firmly as possible on the floor.

Key Coaching Points: Block Tackle, Open Stick

- Adopt the basic grip.
- Do not bend your knees, or plant your feet too early; keep mobile.

The block tackle. (a) The defender closing down to make the block tackle. (b) The defender making a successful block tackle.

- Take a sideways position, with left foot in front of right foot.
- The stick should be at right angles to the line of the ball.
- Use the whole stick for the block, including the shaft.
- When you have won the ball scan for passing options and outlet the ball.

Block Tackle, Reverse Stick

To use the reverse stick you will almost definitely have to rely on a strong left hand as you may not get the chance to get the right hand on the stick without losing balance and reach.

With your left hand at the top of the stick and the point of the stick towards the ground, keep your stick low and in front of your body with the head of the stick forwards of your left hand for strength.

This angle of the stick will make it more difficult for the attacker to break through. The stick should also be angled so that the top edge is forward of the bottom edge. In this way if the ball makes contact with your stick in the tackle it will wedge between your stick and the surface. When committing yourself to this tackle, if you are eliminated you will have little chance of recovering so make sure that you work on your timing to increase success.

It is probably a good idea to wear a glove on your left hand to protect it. There are many variations of gloves that you can use.

Key Coaching Points: Block Tackle, Reverse Stick

- Use a one-handed grip, left hand.
- Extend the stick in the left hand.
- Make the tackle at the last moment.
- Lay the stick flat on the ground.

- Use the whole stick for the block, including the shaft.
- When you have won the ball, drag to open stick side.
- Scan for passing options and outlet the ball.

Tackling, channelling and intercepting are important skills in the defenders' tool bag and from these skills come exciting opportunities to start the next attack. Rarely will you find yourself in an ideal position and therefore concentration and early preparation will help you in winning the ball back for your team. Balance and timing are key defensive abilities and these can be developed on the practice ground. Match play situations will help this process.

All players need to develop their ability to read the game and make interceptions, work on your team skills and defend together as a team; this will undoubtedly improve your chance of gaining possession and winning matches.

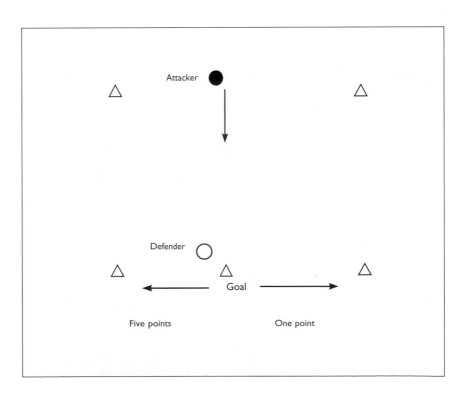

Defending drill for positioning and tackling.

CHAPTER 10

GOAL SHOOTING AND GOAL SCORING

The most exciting part and crucial part of a game of hockey are shots on goal and goals scored. Without these the game would lack dynamism and fun.

There are many aspects to consider when shooting at goal, including entering the circle at the best possible angle to give yourself the best chance to score, placement (often more useful than powerful shots), precise skill execution and choice of shot. These are the keys to success.

Ideally you should try to enter the circle in the best possible position, this position being the middle of the circle where you will have the best angle of shot at goal.

The wide circle entry cannot be avoided but is a lot less dangerous to the opposition as your shot will be from an acute angle and passing options can be minimized.

If you do find yourself running along the baseline you should look to pass to the penalty spot for a teammate to convert into a shot, or encourage a defender to come towards you to tackle and hope that an angle opens up.

Placement versus Power

A common error that players make when they are entering the circle is to believe that their aim is to propel the ball as hard as possible towards the goal, only to often see their shot miss the target, going over the crossbar or by the post.

Power is useful but placement is critical. A shot on target has to be saved and if it is not a goal results. You need to shoot quickly to avoid being tackled first. You should also prepare outside the circle so that you can send the shot before you are tackled. By shooting on target there is also

the possibility of a rebound and this could also be converted into a goal.

Becoming a Goal Scorer

If you want to become a goal scorer there are a number of attributes that you need to develop. You need to be alert to any possibility of a shot. Players need to be able to score from wherever the ball falls around the body. Therefore they need a range of skills to enable them to do this.

It is vital that players scan frequently in the circle so that they can see the goal, and keep a picture in their mind of where the goal is while their attention is on the ball, and read the defenders' position. In the circle the defenders are constantly trying to front and side mark so that they can beat the attacker to the ball. Therefore, passes need to be played away from the defender. Players need to practise these techniques in all areas of the circle. Very few goals are scored from the perimeter of the circle. It is good coaching technique and good player practice to try and finish off drills with a shot at goal.

Attitude

You must be very determined to score the goal. You need to have a winning mentality and improve and increase your ability to make the correct choice of shot in a pressured environment.

Skills

Good ball collection skills under pressure are crucial to the goal scorer. If you cannot

collect the ball you will not be able to have a chance of shooting. Be very aware of the position of both teammates and opposition as this will aid your decision making. Always know where the goal is. Quick hands and quick feet will help you with your choices, your shot and skill execution.

Hitting

If you are hitting the ball at goal you can rarely afford the time you would have at a free hit. Therefore you should work on sliding your left hand down your stick to meet the right hand which will shorten the back lift. In this way you will get the shot away quickly. This may not feel natural but as with all techniques the more you practise the more natural it will feel.

Placement

Good goal shooting is always about accuracy and placement. A shot in target has to be the aim of every goal shot and with that comes a save or a rebound. If the shot is on target and the goalkeeper effects a save the attacking team will have further shots that they may be able to take.

Footwork

Good footwork can make the difference between a good skill and a wasted opportunity. Footwork is the area that all players can work on for all skills and should not be neglected. If you get your footwork correct you will be able to go for power and placement. When you have collected the ball, keep your stick on the ball and move your feet into the best possible position to execute the shot. Although ideally you would want to line up your feet and body as you would for a pass, you may have to compromise this in the shooting area and you should learn to shoot from a variety of positions.

The Shots

All shots are executed in the same way as passing skills. The only difference is when you are shooting your target is the goal whereas when you are passing, the target is the teammate. The shots that we are going to focus on are:

- the hit
- the clip hit
- the push
- the squeeze
- the chip
- the sweep, open stick and reverse stick
- the flick, open stick and reverse stick
- deflections
- rebounds.

The Hit

Hitting the ball gives greater power over a longer distance. It can help change the point of attack for your team and out-manoeuvre the opposition. You should be able to hit off either foot, left or right, but in general it will be with your left foot forward. By transferring the weight from your back foot (right) to your front foot (left) you should get maximum power (see The Hit in Chapter 7).

Key Coaching Points: The Hit

- Try to maintain a sideways posi-tion with your left shoulder pointing towards the target.
- Make sure your body is in a strong position so bend your knees and lower your centre of gravity.
- Try to make sure that as you hit the ball, it is level with your left foot.

- Make sure your hands are together on the stick so that you can make them work together.
- Look at the back of the ball all the way through the action – which means you will keep your head down.
- Follow through towards the target transferring your weight through the ball in the direction of where you want the ball to go.

The Clip Hit

In a tight situation you should be able to use a clip hit to shorten the length of the stick: instead of sliding your hands together at the top of the stick you should slide them together part way down the stick. The key factor is to make sure that the hands work together on the stick and not separately, working against each other.

Key Coaching Points: The Clip Hit
As for The Hit except:

- The left hand slides down the grip to meet the right hand.
- Use a shorter backswing with an emphasis on cocking the wrists (that is, flexing the wrists to about 45 degrees).
- The position of the ball is level with the left foot on impact.

The Push

This is a good technique to use in a tight situation as the stick does not leave the ball until the shot has been executed. This

The attacker about to hit the ball at goal.

A reverse stick hit at goal.

makes it difficult for the opposition to steal the ball from you. Because there is no backswing involved, the push is quickly executed in a tight area, and also offers a high amount of deception that the opposition will find difficult to read. The keys to delivering a good push are quick footwork and, ideally, having your body in a strong delivery position. This will be determined by the amount of time you have. In a situation where you have plenty of time, quick footwork will get your body lined up correctly: the left foot forward, pointing in the direction of the shot.

The strongest position for passing or shooting is a left foot forward, sideways position, so the right foot is behind. The weight is transferred from the back foot (right) through the shot onto the front foot (left). This should give good contact

of the stick on the ball, and whilst power is not crucial, it always helps (see The Push Pass in Chapter 7).

Key Coaching Points: The Push

- The grip is with the left hand at the top of the stick and the right hand further down the stick for control.
- The stick starts in contact with ball and only leaves contact once the shot has been executed.
- There is no backswing.
- Adopt a low posture and follow through to the target.
- Transfer weight from the back foot (right) through to the front foot (left).
- Use quick footwork throughout.

The Squeeze

This is a difficult shot to get right, but if you can master it, you will bring a deceptive and raised shot into your repertoire. The squeeze shot is executed with the downward action of your stick on the ball. The ball is positioned slightly behind your back foot. The downward action of the stick will squeeze the ball into the ground to force it into the air. Your swing will be from above and slightly behind the ball, with your stick making contact with the upper back part of the ball.

Key Coaching points: The Squeeze

- The grip is hands together at the top of the stick, or down the handle.
- Have the ball behind the back foot.

- Point your shoulder at the target, in a sideways position.
- Keep your arms and stick in the same plane.
- Hit down hard on the top/back of the ball.

The Chip

The chip shot at goal is a raised hit, usually achieved with a short backswing. For the chip shot, you need to angle the face of the stick backwards. The ball will be slightly further forward than for the hit and you should try and hit the bottom of the ball. The biggest drawback of this shot is that it is difficult to control and often misses the target, not leading onto a second phase shot (rebound).

Key Coaching Points: The Chip

- Grip hands together at the top of the stick.
- Have the ball in front of the lead foot (usually the left foot).
- Hit the bottom of the ball.
- The position of the ball and the stick angle determine the height reached by the ball.

The Sweep Shot

In a shooting situation where more power is required than a push, then you should use the sweep or the slap. The hit would give you more power but you would need more time to get into the correct body position and execute it.

The sweep or slap can be played with hands apart or hands together, although to put deception on the pass it is probably better to have your hands together on the stick. The body position is sideways, the same as for a hit or push shot. The stick is then taken back along the ground in a large circular action. The ball is often slightly further away from the feet than for the hit. In the attacking circle you can angle your stick slightly backwards at the point of contact, thus lifting the ball.

Key Coaching Points: The Sweep

- Grip either hands together at the top of the stick or hands apart, as in the push.
- Move the stick away from the ball in a large circular action along the ground.
- Adopt a low posture and follow through to the target.
- Contact the ball on the shaft just above the head of the stick.

The Flick Shot

This can be an extension of pushing as the preparation is just the same. The stick starts in contact with the ball and if you recognize a space over a horizontal stick or goalkeeper, you should angle the stick head to lift the ball into the goal. Ultimately you should be able to generate the same amount of power for a flick as you do for a push at goal with some disguise, as at the last minute you would alter the angle of the stick head underneath the ball.

Key Coaching Points: The Flick Shot

- Grip the top of the stick with the left hand with the right hand further down the stick for control.
- The stick starts in contact with ball and only leaves contact once the shot has been executed.
- There is no backswing.
- Adopt a low posture and follow through to the target.
- Transfer weight from back foot (right) through to front foot (left).
- The stick is angled under the ball and the pushing action is upwards through the ball to the target.
- Use quick footwork throughout.

Reverse Stick Flick Shot

This is a difficult shot to execute with power. The key to this shot is placement and surprise. The goalkeeper will not be expecting a shot from this position.

With the ball on the left side of the body, turn your body to face the ball, follow through towards the goal with your right hand pulling up quickly.

Key Coaching Points: Reverse Stick Flick Shot

Coaching points are the same as for the flick shot, except:

- The ball is only very slightly outside the right foot.
- The stick is under the ball.
- The right hand pulls up quickly and towards the target.

Deflections

Deflections are one of the key methods of scoring in the modern game. The aim of the team is to hit the ball into the shooting area hard and flat, that is, on the ground. When the forwards do not have time to collect the ball their aim is to allow the ball to run off the face, head or shaft of the stick towards the goal.

One of the key tactical objectives is to make the goal wider by shooting wide of the posts and having a forward on either post looking to deflect the ball into the goal. The forward can control the deflections by the angle of their stick and whether it is high or low. The aim is to run in front of the defenders or goalkeeper and deflect the ball past or over them into the goal. It is a very spectacular goal when it works and is very much a team goal as the key factor is often the hit into the shooting area.

Key Coaching Points: Deflections

- Be brave: run into the line of the ball.
- Depending on which side the ball is coming and the goal angle, position your stick either open or reverse so that the deflection will send the ball goalwards.
- You can use the head or the shaft of the stick.

The flick shot (a) Feet preparation. (b) Setting the base. (c) The base. (d) The execution. (e) The follow-through.

Rebounds

A rebound occurs when the goalkeeper stops the ball from entering the goal and it rebounds off their pads or kickers back into the shooting area. This is also a key method of scoring following a shot at goal. All attackers should be following into the goal area when a shot is made to be ready to execute a second shot if a rebound occurs. Even if you are not shooting you need to be alert to the possibility of a re-bound following a shot. Rebounds tend to reflect a goal scorer's attitude as much as

their ability. Quick reactions, quick thinking and quick decision making single out for-wards with good rebound skills. It requires willingness to get into the danger area and respond to anything that falls near you. Be prepared to improvise.

Key Coaching Points: Rebounds

- Prepare early with both the body and the stick held low.
- Expect every ball to come to you.
- Be prepared to improvise.

Goal scoring is certainly one of the fun aspects of hockey. Try to keep the skill execution as simple as possible. Make sure that you practise in a pressure situation once you have learnt the skills. The simple things need to be done well; if you have time make sure you collect the ball before you think about your shot, but for all shots pre-scan and check for your options for the best opportunity before you are under pressure and the ball is coming towards you.

Attackers in key areas for deflections and rebounds.

CHAPTER 11

GOALKEEPING

Goalkeeping Equipment

It is very important for a goalkeeper to be well protected. A goalkeeper should have the following equipment:

- a helmet
- a throat protector
- a chest protector
- arm guards
- left and right hand protectors
- groin/pelvic protector
- padded shorts
- kickers
- leg guards
- hockey stick
- different-coloured shirt.

It is always useful for a goalkeeper to carry some spare straps, tape and a different-coloured shirt in their kitbag too.

Warm-Up For Goalkeepers

The warm-up is just as important for goalkeepers as it is for field players. They need to do some warm-up activities both before and after padding up. Allow at least an hour prior to practice or a game to accommodate all this.

Physical Warm-Up (20min)

This comprises:

- Steady state aerobic activity 3–5min (running)
- Dynamic flexibility (5–10min)
- Ladder drills (5–10min)
- Sprint drills (3–5min).

Dynamic flexibility drills are available from the National Governing Body. Alternatively, SAQ International produce hockey-specific dynamic flexibility programmes and full training solutions. See www.saqinternational.com

Kitting Up (10–15min)

Technical Warm-Up (20min)

This comprises:

- Low intensity kicking or shooting
- Low intensity hand work
- Intermediate intensity combination work
- Set plays and/or corners
- High intensity shooting and/or game play.

Goalkeeping Skills and Techniques

The Ready Position

Ready position is the stance a goalkeeper takes when the opposing team is on the attack and has the possibility of a shot at goal. From this position the goalkeeper should be able to move quickly in any direction and be able to save, clear and recover. When making a save, goalkeepers are looking to not only stop the ball from going into the goal but also to clear it away from the goal and attackers. If they are unable to clear they need to be able to get into a position to save any rebounds.

Each goalkeeper will have a slightly different ready position but here are some common points that all goalkeepers should use.

The Lower Body

- The goalkeeper's weight should be on the balls of the feet.
- The feet should be approximately shoulder width apart.
- The knees should be slightly bent, just forward of, or over, the knees.
- The waist is also slightly bent, so that the head and chest are over the knees.
- A good saying is 'Head over knees over ankles' (HOKOA).

The Upper Body

With the upper body there can be a lot of variation as to where the goalkeepers

> **TOP TIP**
>
> HOKOA
> Head Over Knees Over Ankles

hold their arms. Some keepers hold their arms out to the sides with gloves pointing up, whilst others prefer to keep their arms lower with gloves pointing down.

A goalkeeper's ready position should be one of preference and it may take a little while for them to find out what works for them.

There are some general points, though:

- Arms and hands should be forward of the chest and shoulders.
- Hands should be above the waist and able to move up or down at speed.
- The stick should be angled forward so that if the ball hits it, the ball will be deflected forward of the goal.

The ready position with a goalkeeper ready to react.

Goalkeeper movement

A key skill in goalkeeping is recognizing the angles you need to know. Goalkeepers need to develop an understanding of where to stand in relation to where the attacker is shooting from. The aim is to give the attacker the smallest view of the goal. The movement of the goalkeeper to position and cover these shots is known as covering the angles.

Goalkeepers need to get behind the line of the ball. They should be able to draw an imaginary line from the ball through the goalkeeper to the centre of the goal-line.

When moving short distances the goalkeeper should move with short side steps working on an arc from one post to the other post maintaining the angles and getting into the ready position.

The goalkeeper needs to continually realign themselves by using the penalty stroke spot and narrowing down the attacker's shot on goal.

Goalkeeper showing the HOKOA position.

How a goalkeeper can use positioning to narrow the angles and cover the goal.

ball hit your foot and bounce off. There is danger on hard shots that young goalkeepers will allow this to happen as the kickers offer great rebound ability. For most shots a goalkeeper has time to assess the shot and control it.

Basic Kick: Save and Clear

This kicking technique is used when the ball is going wide of your feet but not wide enough that you have to stretch to get to it. The aim is to save and clear the ball wide in one action and not just to let the ball hit your kickers and rebound off.

Preparation

- You are in the ready position.
- Keep your head steady in line with the ball.
- Assess the ball's direction towards you.
- Determine your target.
- Keep your eyes focused on the ball.

Execution

- Lead with your head.
- Step towards the ball with your non-kicking foot in line with where you want the ball to go.
- Kick with the instep of your foot as this gives you more control.
- Keep your head and chest over the ball when kicking to keep the ball on the ground.

Follow-Through

- Swing through with your kicking foot in line with where you are clearing the ball to.
- Keep your head over knees over ankle: HOKOA.
- Follow the ball with your eyes.
- Return to your ready position.

Lunge Save

This technique is used when the ball is going wide of the goalkeeper at a fast rate, which does not allow the goalkeeper time to get behind the ball. It is usually a reflex save, and so it is important to time it well.

Depth

Another aspect of covering angles is depth. The further out from the goal you are, the more area you can cover; however, you have less time to react to a shot. How far out a goalkeeper plays will depend on their reaction skills and also their height. For example, a shorter goalkeeper may need to play further out from the goal to cover the same area as a taller goalkeeper.

Kicking

This is a proactive skill that uses three main techniques. It is not just letting the

Basic kick preparation.

Basic kick execution.

Basic kick follow-through.

The lunge kick.

Preparation

- Position yourself between the ball and the goal, while checking your angles.
- Get into the ready position.
- Assess the ball direction.
- Keep your eyes on the ball and head steady.

Execution

- Lead with your head.
- Lunge your foot/leg in the line of the ball.
- Transfer your body weight on to the saving leg.
- Keep your head as far as possible over your lunging knee.
- Contact the ball with the inside of the foot or leg.
- If possible, time the lunge so the momentum is going forward so the ball is cleared away.
- Angle your foot to deflect the ball away from the goal towards the side-line.

Follow-Through

- Push up into the upright position after contact.
- Clear the rebound and deal with the second phase if there is a need to do so.
- Return to the ready position.

Aerial Hand Saves

Generally hand saves are made when the ball is above waist height or you are unable to get to it with your feet or legs. However, the rules concerning the use of the hands have changed since the start of the season 2007/08 and goalkeepers are still coming to terms with what they can and cannot do.

Rules Interpretation

Goalkeepers are permitted to move the ball away with either their hand, their hand protector, arm or body, as part of a goal saving action.

- This action is permitted in all situations where attackers have an opportunity to score or attempt to score a goal, so it can also be used to deny attackers the possibility of possession of the ball or another shot at goal.
- There is no requirement that the ball is going towards the goal when using this action, so a goalkeeper may intercept a pass across the

face of the goal or sweep the ball away from in front of an attacker's stick – there only needs to be the threat of an attacker being able to play the ball. Goalkeepers therefore must not intentionally propel the ball over long distances with their hands. Goalkeepers who propel the ball forcefully in this way (when there is no chance of an opportunity for

The hand save.

the attackers or after a pass from a teammate, for instance) should be penalized with a penalty corner.

- The distance that the ball can be moved away is not specified; however use common sense in judging the distance the ball may travel from the goal saving actions as indicated in this rule. Be aware that the nature of the materials from which the protective goalkeeping equipment is made will have an influence on this. The permitted action is subject to the usual danger considerations.

So with the new rule, goalkeepers can now push their hands towards the ball to save, instead of having to wait for the ball to meet the glove. However, this does not mean a goalkeeper can punch the ball clear with their glove like a football goalkeeper. It just means they can push the ball away as long as it does not put any other player in danger.

To clear most aerial shots it is best either to deflect the ball wide, over the backline, or tip it over the crossbar.

Preparation

- Get into line so that you are covering the angles.
- Get into ready position.
- Focus on the ball and keep your head steady.
- Assess the direction, height and speed of the ball.

Execution

- For balls above elbow height, turn the hand to have fingers facing up; for balls below elbow height turn the hand to have fingers facing down.
- Step towards the ball.
- Make sure the hand is behind the line of the ball.
- Push the ball away with your glove, or stick and glove, as wide as possible.
- For hard shots angle your glove, or glove and stick, to deflect the ball wide and down or up and over.
- Make sure you don't swat at the ball.

Follow-Through

- Maintain your body balance.
- Keep your eyes on the ball if possible.
- Return to the ready position.

Defending a Penalty Corner

Penalty corners are described in Chapter 2.

For a penalty corner to be awarded there must have been a foul within the shooting area or a deliberate foul in the attacking 23-metre area. It is important to remember that the corner is designed to give the attacking team a very good chance to score. A well-taken penalty corner should result in a goal. However, the goalkeeper can do a number of things to make this as difficult as possible. The rules and knowledge of penalty corners are important for the goalkeeper to learn. (see Chapter 14, Set Pieces).

Here are the rules and standard procedure for a penalty corner.

- The defending team are allowed five defenders who start behind the goal-line.
- The ball is placed on the goal-line, 10 metres from the nearest goalpost.
- The player injecting the ball must have one foot outside the field of play throughout the injection.
- The other attackers are not allowed inside the shooting area until the ball is played.
- The goalkeeper must stand with both feet on or over the goal-line and must not leave the goal-line or move either foot until the ball has been played.
- The player injecting the corner has to wait until all the defenders are behind the goal-line.
- The ball must be controlled outside the shooting area before it is moved into the area and a shot is taken.
- The first shot at goal must cross the goal-line at backboard height (18in) therefore it cannot be undercut.
- The shot, if it is flicked, can go into the goal at any height.

- The defenders can leave the backline as soon as the ball is put in play.

There are various ways of defending a penalty corner. It also differs between the men's and the women's game. In the men's game there is a greater occurrence of the drag flick though this is now increasing in the women's game. Therefore the goalkeeper has to prepare for a strike, hit or push at goal as well as being able to react to a drag flick. The goalkeeper should remain poised in the ready position at the point of impact, making sure that their body weight is going forward. Once a goalkeeper has developed their movement and confidence it may be possible to learn a smothering of the ball.

Where possible goalkeepers should stay on their feet as long as possible as this means they can react not only to first phase shots, but also to second phase shots after a rebound.

Young goalkeepers should seek out goalkeeper-specific coaches who have a greater depth of knowledge for developing goalkeepers.

Defending a Penalty Stroke

It is important to remember that the stroke is designed to give the attacking team a very good chance to score. For a penalty stroke to be awarded there must have been a serious foul. A well-taken penalty stroke should result in a goal. However, the goalkeeper can do a number of things to make this as difficult as possible. Defending a penalty stroke is one of the most difficult things for a goalkeeper to do. It is important for the goalkeeper to learn the rules and have a good knowledge of penalty strokes (see Chapter 14, Set Pieces).

Rules and Standard Procedure For a Penalty Stroke

- All other players should stand outside the 23m line.
- The ball is placed on the penalty spot.

- The player taking the stroke must stand behind the ball and within playing distance before beginning the stroke.
- The goalkeeper must stand with both feet on or over the goal-line and must not leave the goal-line or move either foot until the ball has been played.
- The whistle is blown when the player taking the stroke and the player defending it are in position.
- The player taking the stroke must not take it until the whistle has been blown.
- Both players cannot delay the taking of the stroke.

- The player taking the stroke cannot feint at playing the ball.
- The player taking the stroke must push, flick or scoop the ball and is permitted to raise it to any height. As a drag flick is one where the feet start ahead of the ball a drag flick is not used as a skill at the penalty stroke.
- The player taking the stroke must play the ball only once and must not subsequently approach either the ball or the player defending the stroke.

There is no set way for a goalkeeper to defend a stroke. Here are some tips for saving a stroke.

- Stand on the balls of your feet, with your heels over the line.
- Remain balanced with your arms up and ready.
- Try to make yourself look as big as possible.
- Don't try to guess where the attacker is going to put the ball; instead look for cues such as the angle of the stick, position of the feet, but remember the attacker is trying to be tricky.
- When the whistle blows commit and go for it.

The goalkeeper saving a penalty stroke.

Chloe Rogers protecting the ball against the South African challlenge. GB v South Africa, Setanta Trophy, 12 June 2008, Dublin, Ireland. (Photograph supplied by England Hockey, © Adrian Kerry)

PART 3

TACTICS

CHAPTER 12

ATTACKING PRINCIPLES

Once you have learned the basic technical skills, the key factor in playing good hockey is being able to apply the technical skills to game play. One of the key situations to try and create during play is when there are more of your team near the ball on the pitch than the opposition, in other words, you have an overload situation. This means you will have more options and more chance of success than the opposition. Your team will therefore try to create situations where two play one, three play two, four play three, and so on: where your team has more players than the opposition.

Following on from this, each player should have a good understanding of the basic principles of attacking play. A thorough working knowledge of the factors involved will help you experience more success. The main considerations of attacking play are:

- width and space in attack
- support and depth in attack
- penetration including change of pace
- mobility in attack.

Width and Space in Attack

Width is the space between the players across the pitch. All players must be aware of the consideration of width and be prepared to use it. This means every member of the team, because when your team have the ball, you are all attackers, not just the forwards but also the midfield and defenders. All players need to create width in attack, because:

- It gives them more working space in which to exercise skills.

- It provides more and easier one-to-one play situations.
- It reduces the defenders' ability by stretching them, and creates holes in defence, called space.
- It makes the defenders' work much harder as they have more space to cover.

Practice: three against three

Rules and Conditions

The pitch is one-quarter of a normal pitch with goals some 15–20m (12–17yd) wide. With three players on each side a goal is scored when the ball is carried over the goal-line.

Objectives in Attack

- An attacker who is not in possession of the ball must find space on the pitch so the attacker with the ball can either make the pass or drive into the space created.
- To attack in a triangular formation ensuring width and depth. Try not to play in a straight line with your teammates.
- Whilst in possession of the ball, keep scanning to analyse the position of teammates and the opposition.
- Try to disguise the next pass or move.

Objectives in Defence

- To ensure width and depth in defence so as to cover the whole goal, and cover the player who is defending against the attacker in possession. This means defending in a triangle.
- Try to anticipate the moves of the attackers.

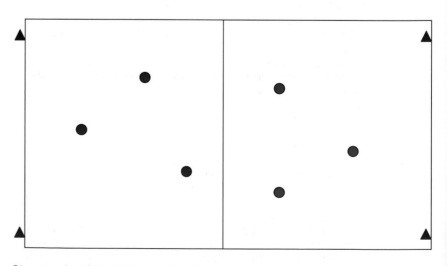

Diagram to show three-against-three with wide goals.

- Delay tackling until you have a teammate to support you.

Support and Depth in Attack

Support and depth in attack is measured by the support offered both in front, alongside and behind the ball. If a forward move is blocked, support from behind the play can link the ball into a new attack.

However, support can come from in front with an attacking teammate stretching the game and then running back towards the ball carrier to offer a pass to them. This is called posting up.

Posting Up (see photos on page 78)

The recipient ahead of the ball carrier leads back towards the ball and receives it in an open stick position, before peeling strong and turning anti-clockwise to face forwards.

Key Coaching Points

- The lead back towards the ball needs to be dynamic, over not too great a distance and the lead must be correctly timed.
- The recipient should only lead back towards the ball carrier at a time when the pass can be made. This will be at a time when the ball carrier has the ball on the end of their stick, is looking in the direction of the posting-up player and can make an immediate pass.
- The lead should not take the player too close to the ball carrier. If it does, it is vital that the player does not then stand still and they should recognize that they might not be in a position to receive a pass so they should clear the space. In doing this, they will either take their marker with them and open up a channel into which a second posting player

may appear, or find themselves in space and therefore available.

- The receipt on the forehand must be strong with the right hand low on the stick, with the player balanced and with a strong body position. While the receipt should be mobile, the player should slow down prior to gathering the incoming ball. This makes a clear difference in the post-up element and the receipt element of the process.
- Upon receipt, the player should peel strong (right to left) to gain forward vision. The peel should first take them back down the line on which the ball came in and then take them on a wide arc. In doing this they will put their body between the player marking them and the ball. They will take the ball beyond the left foot of the player marking them, opening up passing and dribble lanes. They will also buy time for teammates to get ahead or overlap.

A Simple Posting-Up Drill

- Start with two balls in play, one from either end.
- Two central players post up back towards the passers at the same time.
- Central players receive the incoming ball, peel strong and pass the ball on.

As the players become more adept, then one of the two central players can be a defender and the drill can be reduced to one ball with some pressure put on the receipt.

Screened Receipt

A different lead that a player might use when receiving a ball from behind is a screened receipt. In doing this, they seek to protect the incoming ball by putting their body between it and the defender.

While it could be argued that posting up would achieve this too, the screened receipt differs in that the recipient looks to collect the ball facing forwards and prevent

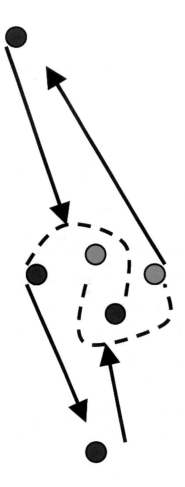

Post-up drill.

the opposition from getting the ball by the way in which they receive it.

Key Coaching Points: Screened Receipt

- As recipient, you must have some angle on the pass; is very difficult to screen receive without this angle.
- Time your arrival into the space in which you want to gather the ball at the appropriate moment.
- Receive the ball in stride and mobile, recognizing that if you arrive too early you must not stand still. By continuing to screen lead, other passing or dribble lanes will be opened up.

Posting-up set-up.

The player offers themselves for the pass.

The player collects and rolls away from the defender.

• Having received, you as ball carrier should straighten up the line of running to fully eliminate the defender.

Combining a Post Up with a Screened Lead

Often sides can be opened up through players leading in opposing ways and through working off one another's leads. A drill can be used to develop this understanding of connections between the ball carrier and more than one lead ahead of the ball.

• The deepest red player (could be the centre half (CH)) is on the ball with two players to their right. One is higher than the other, (could be inside right (IR) and right wing (RW)).
• The IR looks to screen lead on the inside of their opponent, initially with the intention of looking to receive in

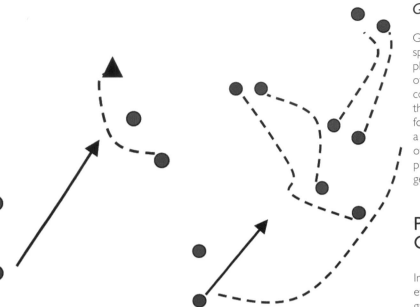

A screened receipt.

Post-up and screened lead.

Getting Ahead

Getting ahead is the action of creating space and leading the decision making of a player in an attacking situation. Being ahead of the ball carrier is not enough, you must continue to work ahead or rotate behind the ball carrier to get free, or create space for the ball carrier. An example would be a RH giving the ball to the IR and then overlapping or cutting inside ahead of the player who has just received the ball and getting ahead of the ball carrier.

Penetration Including Change of Pace

In attack, possession is paramount. However, possession alone will not win you games: goals are required, and goals can only be scored if effective 'penetration' of the defence is achieved.

Penetration is an understanding and application of:

a screened manner and attack the middle of the pitch.

- If the IR leads too early and gets so far infield that there is not sufficient angle for the CH to make the pass, the IR will continue leading, taking their marker with them.
- Recognizing the movements made further down the pitch, the RW posts up into the passing lane created by the movement of the IF and gives the CH a second passing opportunity.
- The initial passer may now take the option to get ahead of the posted-up player on the ball to create a possible overload situation. That said, if this were the CH as outlined in this example, there would need to be further recognition that leaving the middle of the pitch free would expose fullbacks in the event of a turnover.

If this is not possible and the team have stretched the length of the pitch, this would enable the team to work on the principle of getting ahead.

The inside left has given the ball to the centre forward who has posted-up for the ball. The inside forward is then running to get ahead of the centre forward to utilize the space created.

- pace (including change of pace)
- support and depth
- width and space (both creating and using it)
- mobility.

You should also know or recognize that the ball must be played past or behind the defenders. Many teams have good build-up but lack penetration to beat the defenders.

Penetration can be achieved by passing into a space behind the defender, allowing for a forward running onto the ball, picking up in flow. It can also be achieved by creating a two-against-one situation so that you have more options than the defenders.

The main factor in any penetrating move is space. Creating space for yourself or a teammate will quite considerably raise the chances of success of a penetrating move.

Practice: Four Against Four

This is a good practice to use to emphasise this feature of penetration.

Rules and Conditions

Two teams of four players play on one-quarter of a pitch. The aim is to dribble the ball under control across the other team's backline.

Objectives

- To improve penetration of defences
- To improve width of vision
- To give width and depth in attack and defence

- When attacking to recognize and play the ball into space where team-mates can pick up in flow
- To scan to aid recognition of space and opposition
- To be able to make long, straight and deceptive passes
- To move into spaces away from defenders, developing mobility
- To know how to mark an opponent or an area
- To move into space immediately after making a pass.

Mobility in Attack

The pace at which the game is now played means that mobility is a key factor in identifying talented players. Now the game allows multi-substitutions it is imperative that players show mobility. An attacker has to run for most of the time that they are on the pitch, seeking good attacking positions for him/herself or dragging the defenders out of position to make space for the defender's two options:

- to go with the attacker and leave a hole in the defence, or
- to stay in the area and leave the attacker who then becomes unmarked with a possible chance of a shot at goal.

In order to capitalize on the problems this may cause the defence, attacking players must understand:

- how to move to give the best possible support to a teammate who has or is about to receive the ball
- when is the best time to move
- how to move in such a way that if the ball is played to them they are positioned to play the next part of the move
- how to maintain and create space around themselves so the ball can be played to them.

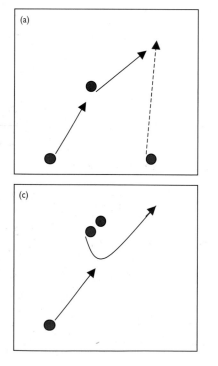

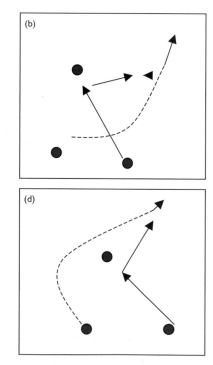

Examples of attacking two-against-one situations. Attackers in red and defenders in blue. (a) Ball carrier travels towards the left foot of the defender and passes the ball to teammate who has run right and ahead. (b) Ball carrier travels from right to left, whilst teammate loops behind them, a short reverse stick pass in to the space created by the angled run, which is picked up by player looping round. (c) Attackers start in a line with the defender; high defender travels back towards the ball carrier (post up); the pass is given to the open stick side and the attacker rolls around the defender with the ball. (d) Ball carrier travels right to left; support attacker gets ahead of the ball carrier and continues their run behind the defender; ball carrier passes the ball into space behind the defender, which support attacker runs on to.

CHAPTER 13

DEFENDING PRINCIPLES

We have just looked at the attacking principles and recognized that one of the key aims of hockey is to score goals. It is vital we now turn our attention to learning how to defend and prevent the opposition from achieving their aim of scoring goals. We have to remember that hockey is a team game and that as individuals we do not have to win the ball ourselves, but rather we have to take responsibility to try and win the ball back as a team, and understand our role in that process.

These are the basic team principles of defence.

- On loss of possession, the nearest player puts pressure on the ball carrier.
- Intercept positions are taken up by potential receivers of passes.
- Players cover space through which the ball can be played.
- Defence try to be as compact as possible to restrict available space.

The main considerations of defending play are:

- covering and delay in defence
- depth
- control, restraint and patience
- balance in defence
- restricting space: closing down and channelling
- zonal defence or marking
- man-for-man defence or marking.

Covering and Delay in Defence

One of the key risk management areas of defending is making sure that you have some cover in defence. Ideally the opposition players will be matched in numbers and the defending team will try and have a spare player who will cover for the other members of their defence. When an opposition player is in attack and has the ball, one of the defenders will engage them and try to delay them purely by their positioning. This delay enables members of their own team to track back at speed and assist by covering the person

The defender in the red shirt has been beaten; the deep defender delays the attacker.

Because the deep defender has delayed the attacker, the beaten defender has recovered to cover for the defender engaging the attacker.

who is about to tackle to try and win the ball. If they don't make a successful tackle then the cover defender can then engage the attacker.

Depth

Depth in defence is part of managing the risk that may be caused by the opposition. As a team it is important that there is some use of different lines of defence. Teams should be careful not to just watch the ball and end up with a straight line of defence. If the defenders find themselves in a straight line then they can be beaten with just one pass. By making sure that you have different lines you should prevent one pass being successful for the attacking team.

Control, Restraint and Patience

As a defender, it is fundamental to show patience. If you rush in it is easier for a skilful attacker to evade you and beat you. Therefore you have to wait until the ball comes off the stick or they make a poor decision. By showing control you will also use your stick in a more sensible fashion and not crash in and hit the attacker's stick and give away a free hit. If you can work as a team it will help with your patience, restraint and control as you will have a joint responsibility to stop the opposition.

Balance in Defence

Balance in defence is a key aim for all teams. The team needs to make sure they cover the width of the field and maintain a depth in covering the area into which the attackers will be advancing. If all the defenders find themselves on one side of the pitch they have lost the balance they are striving for and the opposition will expose their weak areas. Also, if the defenders find themselves in a single line across the pitch, the opposition – if they break this line –

can eliminate all the defenders with one move or pass.

Restricting Space: Closing Down and Channelling

The main idea of closing down and channelling is to dictate to the attacker which space they should use, thereby not allowing the attacker to use any space they determine. This action is known as channelling the player with the ball, and it will give you control of a difficult situation. When channelling you should use the lines of the pitch to assist you and in general you should try to push the player with the ball wide to the sidelines, or the baseline. If you are in the middle of the pitch you would try and channel them onto your open stick side or the open stick side of one of your teammates, thereby making an opportunity for a block tackle. For the technical points of closing down and channelling see Chapter 9.

Generally we want to close and channel onto the open stick where the defence is the strongest. There are, however, circumstances when channelling on the reverse side is required. Examples of this are where the attacker receives on the left of the defender and the defender is not in a position to overtake and force onto the open stick. The other is when there is no defensive cover in place and to force into the open stick would lead to greater danger. This would tend to happen in the defensive inside left channel and that is why the general principle is to force the attacker wide to the nearest wing or side of the pitch.

Interception

The defender needs to be in a position that is ball side of their opponent and which will enable them to see their opponent and the ball. The distance from their opponent will be determined by the distance the ball is away from them

and the opponent. The closer the ball, the closer the defender must be to their opponent. This will also help the defender to provide cover for teammates while still fulfilling their own marking responsibilities. For the key technical points of intercepting see Chapter 9.

Pressing

Pressing is a very aggressive style of defending, which is trying to force turnovers by applying pressure to defenders in a variety of ways.

Coaches often use the words 'half court press' to describe what is merely setting the front line of the defence near the halfway line. A half court press has a very clear structure designed to exert defensive pressure in an aggressive manner. The times you would choose to press would vary but there are key points to note.

KEY POINT

When to press

- When the ball is on the sideline in the defensive 20m (25yd) area. There will be very little room for defenders to outlet the ball from deep defence.
- When we need to get the ball back.
- To keep the ball at the back of the opposition defence to use up time: for example with one goal up and two minutes to play.
- To expose any weak defenders on the opposition.

Zonal Marking or Defence

Zonal marking is another form of defence that some teams will adopt where they will have responsibility for an area of the pitch. The key points box gives the reasons for using this form of defence.

KEY POINT

When to use zonal marking

- Marking an attacker when they come into the individual defender's area of the pitch.
- Passing an attacker on to another defender when they move out of the defender's area of responsibility.
- Covering space through which the ball may be played.

Man-for-man Marking or Defence

Some teams will only ever play a man-for-man marking as they find this an easier way to apportion responsibility. It can have its drawbacks if the opposition are quicker or more skilful.

KEY POINT

When to use man-for-man marking

- For marking the same player wherever they are on the pitch.
- When covering space through which the ball may be played.

Here we see an attacker being marked man-for-man.

The fact that there is no offside in hockey has an effect on teams and their defence. The impact is that teams can be stretched the whole length of the pitch if they defend deep in the opponent's half, and a lot of space can be created. The shooting area can effectively become bigger as attackers can play high on the baseline.

Different Systems of Play

Teams will play different systems to suit a more attacking or defensive style of play.

The systems should be chosen once the strengths and weaknesses of the players are determined. The shape of a system reveals how a team wants to attack or defend. For example, the formation of the forward positions may resemble a forward or a backward arrowhead. The system of play defines each player's positional responsibility. What follows are some of the main systems that are used, with a general explanation of why they are chosen as a system of play.

5–3–2–1 System of Play (see diagram on page 84)

This means five forwards, three half backs, two fullbacks and one goalkeeper.

This is the traditional system employed by many countries including Great Britain, India and Australia. With five forwards, the system was thought to be very attacking and the weaknesses came when the fullbacks found themselves level with each other and lacking cover and depth. The

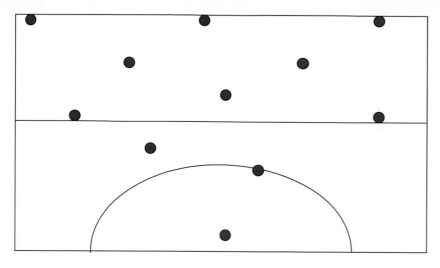

5–3–2–I system of play diagram.

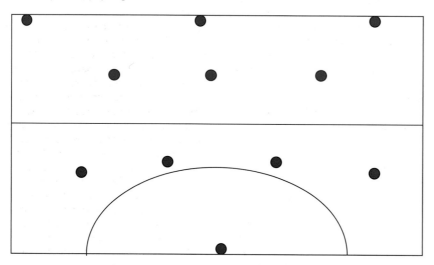

3–3–4–I system of play diagram.

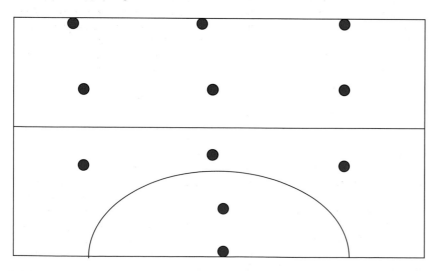

3–3–3–I–I system of play diagram.

opposition could beat the defence with one pass once they were in a straight line.

3–3–4–I System of Play

This means three forwards, three midfielders, four defenders and one goalkeeper.

This system is known as the European sweeper system and provides the team with a number of defenders equal to the opponent's attackers. It also provides the defenders an extra back to provide cover in defence. It is believed that if a team is weaker than its opponent it had to concentrate on defence and even a strong team can benefit from an extra fullback.

Moving forward, the centre half is still attacking, but in defence all ten players retreat. The first line of defence is the forwards who have to track back, channelling and harassing the opposition and this is then replicated throughout the team.

3–3–3–I–I System of Play

This system is one of the more commonly used systems in hockey because in it the players' roles are most clearly defined. There are three forwards, three midfielders, three defenders, one sweeper and one goalkeeper. The aim is to overlap as much as possible from the back three through the midfield. The key to this system is to overload the numbers in attack or defence depending on where the ball is and where the majority of the game is being played.

The game of hockey is won by the team scoring the most goals. In order to do this many teams have built their goal-scoring opportunities on a strong and disciplined defence and it is the application of the defending skills into team tactics that enhances the chances of success. This chapter has tried to help you understand when you should use which technique to aid your team's set-up.

CHAPTER 14

SET PIECES

Set pieces are recognized patterns of play that are used when the ball starts in a stationary position.

Penalty Corners

Penalty corners (see Chapter 2) have over the last few years become a major method of creating the opportunity for scoring goals. Teams have perfected the art of drag flicking and many successful variations. This has increased the likelihood of winning penalty corners during matches, allowing teams free opportunities for the penalty corner specialists to score from the top of the circle.

Mental Preparation

One of the most important facets of developing into a penalty corner specialist, or part of a successful penalty corner team, is a player's mental attitude. Here are a few key points involving successful mental attitude toward penalty corners.

Body Language

It is important when taking penalty corners that the attacking team is confident and displays confident body language to the opposition. This will add to the already pressurized situation that the defence find themselves in. This puts the attack on the front foot and could force basic errors allowing easier goal scoring opportunities for the penalty corner team.

Reading the Defence

Attackers need to try and read what type of defence the opposition will run. If this is predictable then the attacking team can choose the specific variation that will be the most effective against that type of defence. This can be done by looking at the body language of the defence as well as their positions on the line.

Deception

This involves trying to convince the opposition that the attacking team will be trying a certain method of scoring and then in fact they do something completely different. For example, putting two players on the opposition who will be paced to slip, hit or flick the ball passed to them encouraging the opposition to run a two-against-two defence and then sliding the ball right into the space for an easy shot.

Video Analysis

In international hockey, teams have the video facilities to study all movements and variations in the opposing team, which is very important in set pieces for penalty corners. Because of this video analysis, it is very important that players involved in the penalty corner attack always start in the same position on the circle edge, and also use the same body language, whether they are directly involved in the variation or not. This will make it extremely difficult for the opposition defence to read and therefore they will not know which defence to employ. By the same token it is crucial that penalty corner attacking teams study the opposition defence and work out which will be the best opportunity to score.

Rebounds

All players involved need to know exactly what variation is being used each time as this will allow them to be in positions where the most likely rebound will occur. Some teams will actually employ a penalty corner variation where they just strike the ball at 80 per cent at the goalkeeper's pads and then players get in quickly for an easy

flick over the logging goalkeeper. Australia has used this tactic effectively in the past.

Technical Skills

Injection

Injection is the method used to commence the penalty corner, where a player will inject the ball in to the field of play. The technique of injecting at penalty corners is crucial to allowing the players at the top of the circle to achieve a good shot at goal. The push needs to be quick, as the player at the top of the circle then has more time to execute a flick or hit. It also needs to be accurate, so that the player at the top of the circle does not have to move around first before executing that flick or hit.

The pace also needs to be consistent as the player at the top is moving onto the ball at a certain speed, and if the push is suddenly a little slower, then the flicker will get to the ball too early and not be able to execute the shot correctly.

The player's right foot needs to be placed parallel to the baseline just behind the line approximately 20cm (8in) away from the ball on the push-out spot.

The player should then turn their body to face the stopper at the top of the circle and place their left foot pointed just to the left of the target.

The player then places the hook of the stick behind the ball. Once the player is comfortable that the ball is lodged in the hook of the stick then they can look up and face the target. It is crucial that the injector has a low centre of gravity as this will allow the stick to drag the ball forward towards the target. The low centre of gravity will also help generate the power needed to ensure a quick push-out.

The accuracy of the injection is controlled by:

The penalty corner injection, view from the side.   *The penalty corner injection, view from behind.*

- the path the stick follows with the ball all the way to the follow-through
- the right leg of the player following through at the target after the injection.

It is important that the injector tries to make a straight path for the ball from the push-out spot to the target.

If the ball starts on an outward movement and then straightens up, the ball will generate topspin on its path to the top of the circle. This spin makes the job of stopping the ball dead very difficult. If the path is straight or slightly inwards at the start, then it will have underspin on it, which makes the stopping easier.

Stick Stop

The stop at the top of the circle is a very important part of the penalty corner and when executed correctly can make the difference between scoring or not. It is

crucial to ensure the ball is stopped dead as this will allow the flicker/hitter the perfect opportunity to execute their skill. Also, if there is a variation and the ball needs to be moved across the circle, the execution is made a lot easier by the ball being stationary.

Each player has a different way of holding the stick or executing the stop; there are however a few crucial aspects that can be followed in order to ensure consistency.

- The hands on the stick must be relaxed and not too wide apart.
- The player should try and stop the ball as close to the head of the stick as possible. This will make moving the ball for variations a lot easier and the hands will help control the head of the stick when the ball hits it.
- The player needs to cushion the ball into the stick and not push at the ball.

Hit

When the attacker is hitting the ball from the top of the circle the goalkeeper will normally lie down ('log') leaving only a gap at the right of the goal. Normally teams will put a post player in this area to protect against a hit in this area.

The key to making it difficult for the post player is obviously to strike the ball as hard as possible but also to try and lift the ball slightly. The technique for doing this varies depending on the surface you are playing on. When playing on sand based Astroturf the easiest way to lift the ball is to strike it from a position that is slightly ahead of the normal position. By letting the ball roll forward slightly more than normal, the angle of the stick at impact will be slightly angled backwards allowing for the ball to take off above the pitch. This takes a lot of practice and the key is not to let the ball roll too far forward, which could cause the shot to be lifted above the backboard and is also

The stick stop or trap preparation.

The stick stop or trap execution.

extremely dangerous to everybody in the defence.

On water-based Astroturf the technique is much more controlled, and involves striking slightly down on the ball. By striking down into the spongy Astroturf the ball should squeeze up and off the ground. With this technique the shot will not lose any of its speed, and in fact on some surfaces the ball squeezes up quicker than a normal strike. Again this requires lots of practice in figuring out how steeply to swing down on the ball.

Once you have perfected the lifted shot it will allow the striker the option of hitting to the left side of the goal where the goalkeeper will be trying to cover the shot with just their stick lying on the ground, making it a very difficult save.

Drag Flick

In order to drag flick successfully players need to focus on all the following areas.

The practice corner routine of stick stop or trap, followed by the hit.

Footwork

When approaching the ball the flicker needs to make sure their feet are working well. The approach must be comfortable and not too long or too quick. It is all about rhythm; the key is technique rather than the speed at which the flicker approaches the ball. The movement in the approach must be consistent in the build-up to the final skip and placement of the feet to execute the flick. By having a consistent approach you ensure that your feet are in the correct position each time to execute the perfect flick.

The Approach

Every player will have their own preference as to how many steps to take in the approach to the drag flick. The key to getting this aspect right is to make sure you take as many steps needed to get rhythm. However, the fewer steps taken, the less chance of error and inconsistency. The top flickers in the world generally try and start a few yards away and take three steps: left foot, right foot, left foot and the final skip. This is enough to get a good rhythm. The rhythm will also be controlled by the pace of the approach. The key is to start slowly and build up the momentum in the final step and skip.

The Skip

The final movement before landing the right foot into the circle is the skip. There are two ways to execute this and the choice is a matter of personal preference.

Skip forward with the right leg overlapping the left in front.

Skip forward with the right leg behind the left leg.

The Right Foot

It is crucial that the flicker tries to get their right foot as far past the ball as possible. Normally the right foot should land at least 30cm (1ft) inside the circle. This will ensure that the flicker's body is ahead of the ball at pick-up and allow for a long drag along the stick before the ball is released. By landing this far in front of the ball it is crucial that the flicker is in a very low position, allowing both their hands and stick to be low enough to the ground to pick the ball up. Once the stick is in contact with the ball the flicker's body position must stay extremely low with their hands well below the level of the knees. The stick must be as parallel to the ground as is physically possible. This will allow the ball to slide from the head of the stick up the shaft. The idea is to try and get the ball to slide about a few centimetres up the shaft. Once the ball is up the stick, the real acceleration can take place from the body and the hands flicking the ball. The key to generating power is to get the hips and legs through the ball and get a big follow-through with the right leg. Another key point is to get the hands and stick driving up and past the left side of the body.

Left Foot

When in the final phase of execution it is important to try and get the left foot to point towards the goal. A lot of flickers land their left foot towards the corner flag. This does not allow the body to come through with as much power and it could also put a huge strain on the knee joint, and cause injury.

Deception

Goalkeepers are becoming more accustomed to facing drag flickers, so it is an advantage for flickers to use some deception on the execution of the flick. To deceive the keepers the flicker needs to try and make the goalkeeper think that he is flicking the ball to the one side of the goal and then, using his wrists and body at the last second, adjust and flick the ball into the other side of the goal. Keepers will confirm that once their weight is on one foot it is very difficult to change direction and make a save the other way. It is important that the flicker does not develop two separate techniques for the flick to the left and the right. The build-up and pick-up of the ball must be the same, with the slight change all happening in the last stage of execution. By carrying the ball on a straight line at the goal for as long as possible, the goalkeeper will not know which side the flicker is flicking and therefore will not be able to commit early to make the save. This will give the whole side of the goal to flick into, making the save a reflex save as opposed to one that they have anticipated from the flicker's technique.

Tactical Awareness

Most drag flickers, particularly the younger players, want to flick the ball under the roof of the goal. Admittedly this looks fantastic when it works, but the top corners may not always be the most effective area to flick into. Goalkeepers themselves report that often the most difficult height at which to make a save is about 45cm (18in) off the ground. This height is difficult as the keeper is caught between making a save with his feet or his glove, and it is hard for the keeper to get to with either feet or gloves. If you watch the top flickers in the world some of them will flick the ball into the top corners, but most of their flicks will be low where they are asking a lot more of the keeper's ability.

Rebounds

If the attacker has their drag flick or hit saved by the keeper, often the rebound comes into the area that the attacker should have followed through into, somewhere just behind the penalty spot. The attacker must therefore prepare for a first time slap or snap hit. The footwork again is crucial, with the body position being nice and low. Often flickers are bigger players in the team and they need to train for the rebound as it requires quick feet and a quick shot, often first time.

All the attacking players involved in penalty corners need to be well trained in rebounds. Often the goalkeepers will make the initial save and then the ball will be available for a rebound shot. Players need to cover the crucial areas of the circle and be in a low ready position to ensure either a first time rebound or a stop and quick snap shot or flick.

Penalty Corner Defence

It is important that teams have the ability to run different types of penalty corner defences. Doing so will avoid opposition teams reading the defence and then executing the variation that works against that type of defence.

It is also important that the defensive set-up is unpredictable; that means that teams can run all their different defences from the same set-up in the goal. This will also make it very difficult for the opposition attack to read your play and anticipate what defence you will be running.

Mental Preparation

Key members of the penalty corner defence must remain switched on and constantly trying to predict what the opposition attack will be trying. This mental agility will assist the team in deciding what defensive pattern to employ. It will also allow the defence to employ one system and then adjust it slightly as the ball is injected if need be. All players involved in the penalty corner defence need to be very focused on their specific job as the smallest error will create the space needed by the attack to score. It also requires all players to be ready for rebounds if the keeper makes an initial save. The attack will be running in looking for rebounds so it is crucial that even if the option used does not come into your area that you are ready to react to the position of the rebound. You can also be slightly proactive and block the line that the opposition rebounders are running. Putting one's body on the line may make all the difference to preventing a goal being scored.

Technical Preparation

Goalkeeper

The goalkeeper needs to be making the decisions as to which defensive pattern to run and needs to take control of their defensive team. They need to display a confident aura and presence, as this will definitely stick in the mind of the attack before they try and execute the corner.

The initial save has to be the keeper's and they need to ensure that the lines (or 'waves') of defenders are not running in the line of sight. The first wave or line of defence will run ahead of the second line.

Balance is the key to making saves at penalty corners, particularly for flicks. If the keeper is moving then their balance will not be correct, because their weight will be more on one foot than the other. This

A team defending a penalty corner.

will prevent the keeper from pushing off as far as needed in either direction – left or right. Flickers will often try and pretend to flick the ball to the keepers left, thereby enticing the keeper to start moving their weight onto their left foot. Then the flicker uses their wrists to flick it to the keeper's right. As most of their weight is on their left foot it becomes very difficult to push off that leg to make a save on the other side. The keeper needs to make sure they are balanced for as long as possible and make their move as late as possible.

Keepers also need to make decisions on their right-hand side as to whether they should stretch with their feet for a low save or to dive with the stick. The crucial aspect here is the length of the stretch with the leg. If the keeper is tall enough to cover the whole area on the right with an outstretched leg then that is perfect. If not, then the keeper needs to prepare to make a low save using a dive with the stick deflecting the ball around the post.

On the keeper's left, all high saves need to be covered by the left-hand glove and low saves with a left foot stretched save.

If flickers shoot at a height in between, then it is advisable to try and cover the shot with either the feet or the gloves and in some instances both.

First Wave Runner

- **Acceleration**: the first wave runner is normally the quickest player in the team over 10 metres. They must cover the first couple of metres very quickly, so as to attract the attention of the flicker and the attackers and encourage them think that they need to execute their penalty corner more quickly than normal. This will some-times cause enough pressure to rush them and therefore not execute the corner effectively.
- **Pressure**: the main job of the first wave is to create pressure. Very few first waves will be able to prevent the flick/hit so the idea is rather to put the attack under as much pres-sure as possible to try and ensure a poor execution. The line that the first wave runs is also important; it

must not be too wide but rather in the eyeline of the player posing the main threat. Again, this may be the key to just putting the flicker off as he sees the first wave approaching in his line of sight or the line of the flick.

- **Variations**: the first wave runner must not run right past the attack-ing castle. A castle is the group of attackers that constitute the penalty corner attack action, one attacker to stop the ball and one to strike the ball. The player needs to be aware of their role in any variations that are to be played. If the ball is slipped either left or right then they have to stop and drift to either side to ensure there is still pressure on the execu-tion. If the ball is slipped too far to either side then the job of the first wave is to turn and cut the circle so the attack cannot pass the ball across the circle.
- **Stick position**: the first wave needs to be aware of what defence the team is running and vary how they hold the stick accordingly. If the team is using a three-against-one defence then the player can hold the stick in the right hand as they may be required to drift right as the ball is slipped. If the team is using a two-against-two defence then the slip is not the first wave's concern and it is probably better to use the stick in the left hand (still showing the front stick), which allows the player to protect against the slip right. As the first wave approaches the attack, the body position needs to be low to avoid any passes going through them. Most defensive set-ups will allow for passes past the first wave but if it goes through them there will be space for the attack.

Post Player

- **Body position**: the post player needs to identify whether the oppo-sition have more of a threat with a hit or a flick as the body position of the post player will vary accordingly.

- **Defending a flick**: if the attack has a powerful flick then the post player needs to stand with legs slightly wider apart and probably needs to stand in line with the post or even slightly outside to allow the stick to cover the inside of the goal on his right. Standing to the side allows the post player space to see the line of the flick and room to move the arms up or down to make the save. Any touch on the flick usually puts it around the post or over the top.
- **Defending a hit**: if the threat is a hit then the post player should stand with legs close together and inside the post. As shots need to be below the backboard the stick should be held vertically with the head near the player's left foot. The right foot should be in line with the logging keeper's heels and the left foot just inside the post. When the hit arrives the player should just try and glance or deflect it around the post for a long corner. There should be a minimum of movement by the stick.

Second and Third Waves

The roles of these players vary according to each penalty corner and what defensive pattern is called. However, both players must be very aware of all the attackers who may be running in for variations. Defenders need to use their low body positions to move quickly and protect the danger areas as well as to block the attack-ers who are running in.

Rebounds

All defenders need to make sure they are ready for when the keeper makes a save. It is very difficult to predict where the ball will land so the defenders need to be in a low body position to allow for a quick step or two into the space where the ball drops. The low body position will also allow a player to be strong on the ball and protect it from attackers running in. It will also allow the defender to block the attackers running in for rebounds without just getting knocked over.

The players chosen to defend penalty corners need to be strong and tough.

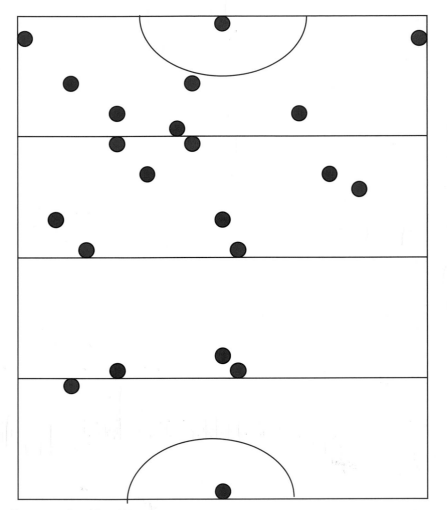

Team set up for a 16-yard hit-out.

explosive and perfectly timed with the player laying the pass. If not then the pass may not find its target and if any pass is intercepted in this defensive area it may lead to the opposition scoring or creating penalty corner chances.

If the team has a player with the technique to execute a big aerial pass then that player can release the pressure by throwing the ball right over the press. In fact the team can use the aerial pass as a set play in order to create a few attacking opportunities. This will, however, require understanding among all involved and perfect timing with the leading of the forwards and midfielders. The player executing the aerial pass needs to also make sure that the ball is landing in a wide area and not in the middle of the field. By landing the ball in a wide area it eliminates the immediate threat of a counter-attack if the opposition receive the aerial pass. In the option below, the space that is manipulated is where the opposition right defender should be. The opposition right defender will be marking the left wing so if the left wing makes a lead towards the ball the right half should follow. This will leave space for the centre forward to then lead in to receive the aerial.

It is important that the players time these leads well. The left wing must only lead towards the ball once eye contact is made with the centre forward. The centre forward needs to make their lead as late as possible to catch unaware the defender who is marking them, thus giving them a few yards to pick up the aerial pass.

Attacking Free Hits Outside the Circle

When teams defend free hits outside the circle they will normally try and get as many of the team back and try and form a wall on the most dangerous pass into the circle. If the opposition put their entire team in the circle then there will be very little space to apply any moves, but a great opportunity to win a corner as there will be lots of feet to find and good opportunities to force a foul or an

16-Yard Set Plays

When taking 16-yard hits it is important that a team has a number of set plays they can call on if the opposition have put a full press on. They have limited the space so an option to exploit this will have to be used.

The best way of avoiding being pressed by the opposition is to make sure all players set up early and once the 16-yard hit

is awarded the team try and get the ball going as quickly as possible. This should be too quick for the opposition to set up their full press, thus allowing space to get the ball out and away from the danger area. This is, however, not always possible and set plays are required to get the ball out of the defensive zone. Below are a few simple set plays that a team can use to get out of a full press by the opposition. Each option can also be used on the opposite side of the field to the one illustrated. The concepts used in each option involve moving one player out of a zone and then leading another into that space to receive the ball. It is vital that all these leads are

They also should be mentally tough with the ability to move quickly to defend space.

obstruction. If the opposition leave one or two players higher in the field then there is a perfect opportunity to try a set play to create a chance to win a penalty corner or get a shot away.

It is important that teams understand that winning a penalty corner can be an easy option to choose and often the best way of getting a free shot at goal. It is a change in mindset but will create lots of free opportunities for your penalty corner specialists to do their jobs.

Penalty Stroke

A penalty stroke is awarded for a deliberate foul inside the circle area or a foul that would have prevented a certain goal, for example, a defender stopping the ball with a foot on the goal-line. The penalty stroke is taken by any member of the attacking team and they have to start from behind the ball. The goalkeeper has to have part of his feet touching the goal-line. When the umpire blows the whistle the attacker

is allowed to push or flick the ball; the attacker is not allowed any back-lift of the stick, so therefore a hit is not allowed.

> **TOP TIP**
>
> Often a hard fast push is more effective than a ball that is lifted to mid-height towards the goal.

A penalty stroke that has been taken to mid-height allowing the goalkeeper to make a save.

A sideline pass during a GBSL match (Great Britain Super League).

PART 4

FITNESS

CHAPTER 15

PHYSICAL FITNESS

The last three chapters focus on the fitness requirements of hockey, injuries to avoid or manage and the food and drink that players should consume.

The game of hockey brings into play all elements of physical fitness, nutrition, and the avoidance or management of injury. High performers in hockey have a good level of aerobic fitness that enables them to last the duration of the game. They make sure they prepare well for each training and match session by warming up and cooling down after each session. They also make sure they feed the body with the correct fuel by what they eat.

Fitness Requirements

The level of fitness you need to play a game of hockey is entirely dependent on the level at which you would like to play. The higher the level of competition, the faster the game will be and the fitter you must be. There are only a few players who are strong in all areas, and if you were to work on only one area then, in the modern game, it should be speed. This is because the game has sixteen players in a squad and they can be substituted on and off as many times as the coach demands during a game.

Fitness in any team sport depends on the 'line' you play in: forwards, midfielders, defenders or goalkeepers. Players in each position have to perform specific skills and this in turn will have specific physical fitness requirements. It would not be making the best use of a player if they had a massive endurance and aerobic capacity but because of a lack of speed never got to the ball first.

Forwards

Forwards need to be able to run at speed so that they can penetrate the opposition defensive lines. They have to do this continually, so a good aerobic base is vital in order to be able to repeat this throughout the game. With this aerobic base the forwards' training programmes should focus on speed and in particular speed endurance. Any long, slow continuous running would be of no benefit to these players as they would rarely operate in this mode, and it would restrict their speed development.

Midfielders

Midfielders are often considered to be the engine room in hockey, mainly because they are expected to support the forwards and the defenders and are the key link players in the team. They will be continually moving, jogging and sprinting. They need high levels of aerobic endurance but should not neglect the development of speed. It is vital that they can break through the lines to set up attacks and also sprint back to deny any attack by the opposition. Speed endurance is a key training aid for the midfield line.

Defenders

Defenders require the ability to keep up with the opposition's dynamic forwards and as a result they will need quick footwork, speed and agility to be able to mark and track back with the opponents. The aerobic base needed for forwards and midfielders is also required for the defenders. So for defenders, footwork and agility must be an integral part of any training programme.

Goalkeepers

The fitness requirements of goalkeepers are very different to the requirements of the rest of the team. A goalkeeper will be expected to make short dynamic movements, so explosive speed and agility are key training areas for the goalkeeper. Aerobic fitness is not a big part of a goalkeeper's training programme but a general level of aerobic fitness will give them a base from which they can develop the specific requirements necessary for goalkeepers. They should also make sure their explosive speed is available both laterally and vertically in order to cover all areas of the goal.

Speed

Having looked at the specific requirements, speed stands out as being fundamental to high performance in hockey. Some players may have explosive speed over a distance of 10 metres whilst others can maintain that speed for a longer period. Both abilities are valuable but the value of each depends on the position you play.

Short, sharp speed is important in the midfield where players need to be able to penetrate the opposition lines in a confined space. The forwards need speed to get away from their opponents and the defenders need speed to catch a breakaway or to cover for their teammates.

The key areas for speed development are:

• the distance covered

- the intensity of effort
- the rest between efforts.

When developing speed the first two to three strides you make are the vital ones. Having this sharp acceleration could make the difference between getting a stick to the ball or being beaten to the ball by your opponent. The intensity of each effort is also critical. To develop speed you must give 100 per cent effort. If you do not then this will compromise the level to which you can improve. Rest is therefore a key part of a speed training session.

Speed Sessions For Hockey

Begin both the foundation sessions and progressions with a dynamic warm-up. This comprises:

- 5min locomotion, joint mobility, 5min dynamic flex (hurdle and non-hurdle), proprioception and balance, neural stretches, foot speed and reactivity.
- Straight line speed drills. Pick three of the following drills, and perform three repetitions of each over 10m (8yd).

Straight Line Speed Drills

- marching
- skipping
- skipping kicking behind, heels hitting body
- straight leg run
- high knee running
- wall drives in press-up position, driver legs as in running
- sprint starts from walking, running, backwards and lying start positions

Foundation Sessions

Complete one or two sessions a week (depending on the amount of hockey you play).

These sessions rely on *quality* not quantity. The rest periods must be adequate to allow you to perform at 100 per cent during each repetition, so do not cut these short. Concentrate on turning and accelerating out of the turn.

Session One

- Sprint 6 × 20m (walk back recovery)
- Accelerate for 5m, maintain for 20m then decelerate within 10m (reduce this down gradually to 5m as weeks go on)
- Sprint 6 × 40m (same procedure as above but greater maintenance distance).

Session Two

- Sprint 6 × 30m
- Walk back recovery. After six repetitions take five minutes rest then do another set.

Session Three

- Sprint 6 × 10m accelerations
- Sprint 6 × 30m sprint as before
- Full recovery between sets and repetitions.

Progressions

Progress to these when you have developed your straight line speed and have done five weeks of the foundation sessions. After this you can then intersperse the progression sessions to add variety.

Session One

- Jump laterally on two feet then accelerate forwards running for 10m
- Walk recovery and repeat, jumping to the other side
- Do eight repetitions then rest for 5min before completing another set.

Session Two

- Jump forwards then backwards before accelerating for 10m
- Do eight repetitions
- Rest for five minutes then do another set. Walk back recovery between repetitions.

Session Three

- Jog 10m to marker/line, turn off marker/line and accelerate for 10m
- Do eight repetitions, slow walk back recovery
- Rest for 5min then do another set.

Aerobic Fitness

The foundation for all of hockey fitness lies in the player's aerobic fitness. All players need this aerobic base so that they can develop other fitness abilities. A strong aerobic base allows you to run for the duration of a game of hockey and helps you recover from the sprints. Fatigue affects the skills you have to perform and therefore a good aerobic base will help you execute your skills with greater consistency and success.

The methods of training generally used for developing aerobic fitness are:

- continuous training
- Fartlek training
- interval-based training sessions.

Continuous Training

Continuous or steady state training involves constant low-intensity activity for longer than ten minutes. Usually for the development of an aerobic base for a team sport, durations of twenty to sixty minutes are optimal. Because hockey is a running based sport, running is the preferred method of training. Cycling and swimming can also be used to improve the energy system.

The continuous nature of this type of training does not replicate the game of hockey, which involves running at various speeds in different directions. Aerobic training should be done in combination with other forms of training.

Because this type of training can impede your speed development it is best to do your aerobic training in the off season period.

Fartlek Training

Fartlek is a Swedish word meaning 'play on speed'. A session is usually continuous but it includes efforts made at a variety of intensities, which more closely replicates the efforts made in a game of hockey.

Many activities can be included in a Fartlek session: agility circuits, various efforts of intensity, including efforts backwards, forwards, uphill and downhill. Implementation of these sessions can be as varied as your imagination allows you, so you can be as creative as your environment permits.

An example of a Fartlek session might be:

- 5min jogging, warm-up, stretch
- 5min continuous running
- 5min: jog 50sec, sprint 10sec (at 85 per cent effort), repeat for 5min
- 5min jogging
- 5min: jog 50m, stride 50m (at 75 per cent effort), jog 50m, stride 50m, repeat for 5min
- 5min jogging
- 5min: sprint 20m; jog backwards 10m, stride 50m, jog 100m, repeat for 5min
- Cool-down, slow jog and stretching.

Interval Training

Interval training involves using higher intensity sprint efforts interspersed with rest periods. Interval training develops:

- the aerobic base necessary for playing team sports such as hockey
- the anaerobic energy system, increasing your ability to perform repeated sprints efforts with minimal rest.

Two concepts have to be kept in mind when developing an interval training session.

- Work done, which is measured by distance or time taken to implement the effort or the intensity of each effort.
- Rest taken between each effort.

The length of an interval session also varies according to the time of year, or the stage and emphasis of the training phase. During the pre-season, longer intervals of 200–300m (or yards) would be used with rest periods of up to two minutes. Sessions closer to the start of the season will require the distances of each interval to shorten with shorter rest breaks. Interval training is the best type of training for conditions that will be met in a hockey match. What follows are examples of various interval training sessions.

Session One: Early Pre-Season, Longer Intervals

- Run 1 × 4min: 1min walk recovery
- Run 2 × 3min: 1min walk recovery
- Run 3 × 2min: 1min walk recovery
- Run 4 × 1min: 30sec walk recovery.
- Run 2 × 5min: 1min walk recovery.

Session Two: Early Pre-Season, Pitch based Fartlek

- Cruise of pitch for two lengths (at 85 per cent pace), straight to five burpees or tuck jumps or squat jumps
- Jog 25m, sprint to 75m, walk to try line, five press-ups
- Walk 25m, sprint shuttle to 50m and back, fast run (90 per cent) through to 75m and walk to the end
- All the previous three sets:

Set one = three repeats performed continuously (twelve lengths of the pitch)
Set two = three repeats
Set three = three repeats. Allow 2min between sets.

Session Three: Mid-Pre-Season, Pitch/Track Intervals

- Run 2 × 400m with 90sec walk recovery between each
- Run 3 × 300m with 60sec walk recovery between each
- 2min walk recovery
- Run 4 × 200m with 45sec recovery
- Run 5 × 100m with 30sec recovery
- Repeat the set once more.

Session Four: Mid-Pre-Season, Track/Pitch Intervals

Use the two sets alternately (see table below).

Anaerobic Ability

Anaerobic or 'without oxygen' exercise requires bursts of energy over short periods. During anaerobic exercise stored fuels such as glycogen provide energy at a fast rate without the need for oxygen. All players need to perform intense physical effort with a lot of stopping and starting, which uses their anaerobic abilities. Goalkeepers in particular may only have a couple of

Set one	Set two
Run 600m (90sec recovery)	Run 500m (90sec recovery)
500m (90sec recovery)	400m (90sec recovery)
400m (60sec recovery)	300m (60sec recovery)
100m (30sec recovery)	50m (30sec recovery)
100m (3min recovery)	50m

match situations where they are directly involved and where they may be asked to work intensely for a short period of time. Therefore it is vital within the training sessions to train the anaerobic system with short dynamic sprints. These short dynamic sprints must be at high intensity.

Agility

The ability to change direction quickly over a short distance is important for forwards as they look to eliminate their opponents and set up chances for goal. Of course as it is important for attackers, it is equally important for defenders who need to re-act to the opponents' forwards. All players will need to work on their footwork and agility to improve their movement on the hockey pitch.

Make the Most of Every Session

To maximize your efficiency and enjoy-ment of the game you can often com-bine your skill practice with your fitness sessions. This will benefit your game because you will become more adept at skill execution when you are tired. The development of fitness is hard work but if you can intersperse it with skill practice it will be more fun.

The modern game has identified the need to show athleticism and agility in all aspects of the game.

CHAPTER 16

COMMON HOCKEY INJURIES

Injury Prevention

The old saying that 'Prevention is better than cure' has never been truer than when applied to hockey. The demands made by the game on the body seem to become greater and greater, and last for longer periods. The human body has the wonderful ability to heal itself, and comes supplied with some spare parts, but it is not a machine: so it is important to do everything possible to prevent injuries.

There are two main causes of injuries in hockey: the direct and the indirect causes.

Direct Causes

These are injuries caused as a result of a fall or a blow. While falling on an Astroturf pitch usually only results in grazes and burns, more serious injuries do occur. A bad landing when you fall can cause dislocation, breaks or ruptures of any limb that is in the way. Unfortunately for us the game of hockey was created using a hard ball, which brings tears to the eyes of the toughest players when they receive a direct hit.

Indirect Causes

Muscular injuries occur as a result of overuse, poor technique, not warming up, under recovery or inappropriate equipment. Indirect injuries occur not only during matches, but also during physical training.

Overuse

A highly repetitive practice such as injecting corners, drag flicking or even hitting can result in overuse injuries. The best way to prevent these is to put a set limit of how many sets will be completed before resting. Always be aware of niggling pain that may herald the start of an overuse injury, and seek medical advice.

Poor Technique

Injuries resulting from poor technique occur because of the unnatural movement that is required from the body when playing hockey. Players should be especially careful when training with weights as poor technique often leads to injury. Poor technique may also result from physical imbalances in your body. For example, lack of flexibility in the hamstring region could result in poor technique of tackling, therefore putting extra strain on the back.

Warm-Ups

A warm-up routine should be performed before all matches and training sessions to prepare the athlete physically and mentally for optimum performance.

The warm-up should consist of three main components:

- low intensity aerobic activity
- dynamic sport-specific movements and/or mobility exercises
- rehearsal of skills.

A player receiving treatment from a physiotherapist.

Some individuals may wish to perform static stretching, although there is no research that suggests this decreases the incidence of injury. The inclusion of static stretching would be to cater for individual psychological need.

The intensity of the warm-up is dependent on the intensity of the training session or match. Before a match or high intensity session there should be a gradual increase in intensity during the warm-up to include maximal efforts.

The length of the warm-up will also depend on the temperature. In cold conditions the aerobic element may need to be lengthened and in hot climates the length of the warm-up may be shortened. Ideally before a match the length of warm-up would be in the region of 45min.

Anyone can direct the warm-up, but each player needs to be educated ultimately to take responsibility for their own warm-up.

During the match adequate time should be given to players on the bench to warm up before playing. Substituted players should perform a cool-down (walk and/or jog) to promote recovery and decrease lactate levels before sitting on the bench.

Cool-Downs and Recovery

Following a training session or match the players need a cool-down to allow the body to recover to a normal resting state. The cool-down consists of three main components:

* low level aerobic activity
* static stretching and/or mobility exercises
* accelerated recovery techniques.

Low level aerobic activity should be undertaken to decrease lactate levels. The length of time for this activity will depend on the intensity of the training session. For high intensity sessions and matches this should be in the region of 8–12min of jogging.

Static stretching or mobility exercises should be undertaken so the muscle returns to normal resting length.

Warm-up examples.

Accelerated recovery techniques such as contrast showers or ice baths may help speed up recovery after training sessions. Contrasting hot (2min) and cold (30sec) showers for three cycles has been shown to decrease post-exercise lactate levels. This technique may help when the active recovery time of the warm down is limited or after speed endurance sessions.

Ice bathing (1–10min) may help decrease muscle damage and stiffness following high intensity sessions (such as sprint or weights sessions). There is no research to indicate the optimum time for submersion,

Stage 1 of the cool-down.

Shin Pads

It is strongly advised that *all* players wear shin pads when playing hockey. It is compulsory to wear them during an international match.

Gum Shield

It is strongly advised that gum shields are worn for all matches and training. For example, it is compulsory to wear them when playing for and training with the England squad. A made-to-measure gum shield from either a dentist or a specialist company like OPRO will provide the best protection (www.opro.com).

Hand Guards

By wearing a hand guard you minimize the very real risk of breaking your hand and ripping your knuckles to shreds.

Stage 2 of the cool-down.

but it will depend on the water temperature and the body composition of the athlete. Ice baths for athletes under sixteen years of age is not recommended without parental consent.

Safety equipment

Hockey is played with a very hard ball, so wearing the right equipment of the highest quality is important to prevent injuries.

KEY POINT

- Listen to your body. Niggles are a warning sign that there is a problem.
- Carry spare gum shields, shin pads and hand guards.
- Warm-ups prepare the body and mind, whilst cool-downs help the body to recover.
- Be aware of potential injury risks, such as from poor technique, overuse and under recovery.

Core Stability and Injury Prevention

Core stability training is essential to hockey performance and injury prevention. The body's core muscles are the foundation for all other movement. If you have a weak foundation or core you cannot build strong movements or forces on top of it, in much the same way that a house will not be stable if it has poor foundations. Core stability involves the muscles not just of your back, but also of your pelvic and shoulder girdles.

In simplified terms we have two types of striated, or voluntary muscles in our body, the mobilizers and the stabilizers.

Mobilizers

These are the muscles that are behind the big powerful movements, for example the quadriceps (quads), which provide power when squatting. These muscles have a high proportion of fast twitch fibres, which means they work maximally and fatigue quickly.

Stabilizers

These are the muscles that control how movement is achieved and maintain posture; for example, when doing a one-leg squat, the gluteals (gluts) work to ensure the hips stay level and the knee doesn't drop in. These muscles have a high proportion of slow twitch fibres, so they work sub-maximally for sustained periods of time. These muscles stabilize the trunk and provide a solid foundation for movement in the extremities.

As in any type of training, in order to train the stabilizer muscles they need to be worked in the same way that they are required to perform. They are muscles that work at low intensity and have a strong endurance base. For example, if training Transversus abdominis (the stabilizing abdominal muscles) by doing sit-ups, their ability to *mobilize* would improve but their ability, for instance, to *control* the trunk while changing direction would not.

These core muscles lie deep within the torso. They generally attach to the spine, pelvis and scapulae. When these muscles contract, they stabilize the spine, pelvis and shoulder blades and create a solid base of support. We are then able to generate powerful movements of the extremities.

Correct training of core stability provides the following gains:

- more efficient use of muscle power as less effort is lost through compensatory movements in the trunk

- increased ability to change direction, as body momentum is controlled
- increased capacity for speed generation
- improved balance and coordination
- improved posture
- reduced injury risk, as poor movement patterns put undue stress on the structures that have to compensate.

> **KEY POINT**
>
> A very high percentage of injuries within hockey are overuse injuries caused by poor biomechanics and core stability.

Key Principles of Core Stability

A core stability (CS) programme should be designed by a physiotherapist with close liaison with strength and conditioning (S&C) staff. The exercises should relate as closely as possible to what the athletes have to do on a hockey pitch and/or in the gym.

It is important to bridge the gap between athletes moving correctly in an exercise environment and the situation when they are actually playing. Physiotherapists and strength and conditioning staff should identify this when they are pitch side at training sessions, particularly for the athletes with poor form. The framework of the programme should be based on aiming to work on generic weaknesses that have been identified in the athlete.

The core stability programme should be customized for individual athletes, and should take in to account individual needs dictated by injury history, results of screening and movement analysis, and specific roles (for example, injectors, drag flickers, goalkeepers). The design of the programme should also take into account what a hockey player has to be able to do functionally, both on and off the pitch, for example weight training to develop their strength endurance.

The core stability programme may be an opportunity to introduce flexibility exercises for those athletes identified as needing to work on this aspect of their fitness.

The core stability programme should be performed all year round.

> **KEY POINT**
>
> - Core stability can help prevent injury.
> - A core stability programme should be designed by a physiotherapist or strength and conditioning coach in relation with the physical demands placed on the athlete.
> - Perform core stability exercises on a regular basis throughout the year to gain maximum benefits.
> - A gym ball can be used to make core stability as hard or as easy as the individual requires.

Injury Management

Every player is likely to sustain some level of injury that will affect his or her performance. On some occasions an injury may be so severe that it demands hospital treatment, but most injuries in hockey involve damage to the soft tissues.

The process of rehabilitation can be a very frustrating time for an injured hockey player. The extent of the injury will dictate how long the injury will take to heal. However severe the injury that has been sustained, the player is encouraged to keep fitness by continuing to exercise but not using the injured area. The physiologist and physiotherapist will work together to design a way in which fitness can be maintained, for example by aqua jogging, cycling and swimming.

Once the injured area has recovered, the physiotherapist will decide if you are fit to train and will conduct a small fitness test to assess whether you are fit to play. It is important not to feel isolated when you become injured. Rehabilitation is a process that focuses on helping the player to regain playing fitness, which involves communication between player,

A soft tissue injury in hockey.

physiotherapist and doctor, and between the physiologist and coach.

Soft Tissue Injuries

Soft tissue injuries are categorized medically as:

- first degree injuries: which are mild injuries, where swelling, bruising and pain are slight and self-treatment is possible
- second degree injuries: which are characterized by moderate swelling and bruising, with pain on any movement; you should seek advice from a doctor or physiotherapist
- third degree injuries: where there is a complete tear of the injured tissue, significant swelling and bruising with severe pain, even at rest; you should seek medical advice as soon as possible.

Self Help

For first and second degree injuries use the PRICE guidelines for the first three days.

This process accelerates the healing process by reducing the inflammation of the injured area. You will be able to recognize the signs and symptoms of inflammation: heat, redness, swelling, pain and inability to have full range of movement in the injured part.

P: Protection
R: Rest
I: Ice
C: Compression
E: Elevation

P: Protection

It is important following an injury to protect the joint from further damage. The use of a brace or strapping will do this. A second injury so soon after the first will extend the period of rehabilitation.

R: Rest

Rest is a major part of injury management. Rest prevents further damage and bleeding and reduces pain. While it is possible to do gentle exercise to the un-injured part, it is advised to avoid strenuous activity as this will increase your metabolic rate, leading to an increase in blood flow and an over-reaction in the inflammatory process. The length of the

rest period will depend on the severity of the injury.

I: Ice

Ice minimizes bleeding, swelling and pain. It should be applied immediately by placing a damp towel containing chipped or crushed ice. Apply for 10min every two hours. Always wrap the ice in a towel as direct contact to the skin can cause ice burns and nerve damage, which are very unpleasant.

C: Compression

This is the most important part of the healing process. A compression bandage will aid the reduction of swelling, which if left around the injury will slow down healing. There is a certain technique to applying a compression bandage so check with your physiotherapist that you have the right technique and are in no danger of cutting off your circulation.

E: Elevation

Elevation of the injured limb above the level of the heart as soon as possible after the injury has occurred will aid venous return and help reduce the swelling. If possible the injured part should be supported on pillows or in a sling.

KEY POINT

- The healing process cannot be rushed. Your body recovers at a set rate. Trying to rush any stage of healing process often results in its delay.
- The medical staff's job is to get players fit to play again. It is in your best interest to listen to and follow their advice as they know what they are talking about. So make sure you are always honest about your injury.
- Use the PRICE guidelines for first and second degree injuries.
- If you are in any doubt about the management of any injury, always seek medical advice.

CHAPTER 17

NUTRITION

As a hockey player it is important that you have a good understanding of the types of foods and fluids you should be taking on board to enable you to perform your best.

The Importance of Fuel

Hockey is a sport that consists of a variety of exercise intensities ranging from sprinting to standing still. Fuel for the bursts of intense activity is provided predominantly by carbohydrate, and fat is used during the less intense parts of the game. Research shows that muscle glycogen is the most important fuel in team sports.

One of the major causes of fatigue during hockey is depletion of muscle glycogen. Studies have shown that the use of glycogen is more pronounced in the first than the second half of the game. Furthermore it is found that players with initially low glycogen stores cover a shorter distance and sprint significantly less, particularly in the second half, than those players with normal muscle glycogen levels prior to the match.

If blood glucose levels drop during the game this may also lead to a loss of concentration and tactical skills, and a deterioration in team interactions.

So carbohydrate clearly plays an important part in the diet of an élite hockey player, but it is also essential to remember that the body needs a total of approximately forty different nutrients for good health so the balance of the diet as a whole must be carefully considered.

The Importance of a Balanced Diet

A balanced diet will provide you with enough energy and nutrients to stay healthy, feel good and perform well in training and competition. Hockey players have different requirements to the general population but essentially the diet should still be made up of foods from the five basic food groups, with greater proportions from some groups because of increased requirements of specific nutrients, especially carbohydrate and protein. The main nutrients provided by the diet are carbohydrate, protein, fat, vitamins and minerals.

A good training diet should provide approximately:

- 60–70 per cent energy from carbohydrate
- 12–15 per cent of its energy from protein
- up to 30 per cent of its energy from fat.

The daily diet should be made up of a selection of foods from each of the five food groups pictured to ensure you consume the correct balance of nutrients required for the body to function.

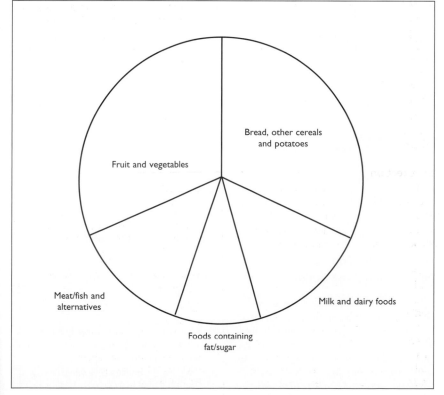

A balanced diet.

Bread, other cereals and potatoes

Fruit and vegetables

Meat/fish and alternatives

Foods containing fat/sugar

Milk and dairy foods

A Brief Guide to the Five Food Groups

Bread, Other Cereals and Potatoes

This group includes bread, potatoes, pasta and noodles, rice and breakfast cereals. It also includes other cereal grains such as oats, maize, millet and cornmeal and other starchy vegetables such as yam and plantain. Beans and pulses can also be counted as part of this group.

The main nutrients provided by this group include carbohydrate, fibre, some calcium and iron plus B vitamins.

To increase fibre intake it is useful to eat wholemeal, wholegrain or high fibre versions of these foods where possible.

Fruit and Vegetables

This group include fruit and vegetables that are fresh, frozen and canned. Dried fruits and fruit juice are also included.

The main nutrients provided include the antioxidant vitamins, C, E and carotene, as well as fibre and some carbohydrate.

Fruits and vegetables also contain other compounds called phytochemicals such as flavonoids (widely distributed in fruits and vegetables), phytoestrogens (soya is a good source) and glucosinolates (found in broccoli, cabbage, cauliflower, brussels sprouts, kale and mustard). These compounds may help protect us against common diseases.

Five portions or more of fruit and/or vegetables should be eaten every day.

Beans, pulses and juices can be counted as part of this group.

Milk and Dairy Foods

This group includes milk, cheese, yoghurt and fromage frais, but not butter, eggs or cream. The main nutrients provided include calcium, protein, vitamin B12 and vitamins A and D. Vitamins A and D are not present in very low-fat varieties. Two or three portions of these foods should be eaten daily.

Lower-fat versions should be chosen where possible, for example skimmed or semi-skimmed milk and lower-fat yoghurts and cheeses.

Meat, Fish and Alternatives

This group includes meat, poultry, fish, eggs, nuts, beans and pulses. The main nutrients provided include iron, protein, zinc, magnesium and the B vitamins, especially B12. You should aim to include two or three portions from this food group every day in your diet.

Lean meats should be chosen and skin removed from chicken to decrease fat intake. Pulses and beans are good alternatives to meat and are naturally lower in fat and also contain carbohydrate and fibre. Oily fish is a good source of omega-3 fatty acids, which can help protect against heart disease and optimize mental functioning.

Aim for a minimum of two portions of fish per week, of which at least one should be oily fish. Oily fish include salmon, trout, mackerel, sardines, pilchards, swordfish, herring, kipper, eel and whitebait. These fish count as oily whether they are canned, fresh or frozen. Only fresh tuna counts as an oily fish, as canned tuna has less omega-3 oil, but it is still a good protein source. Men can have up to four portions of oily fish a week (one portion is 140g/5oz), women two portions per week. Women who are not planning to be pregnant in the future can also have up to four portions per week.

Foods Containing Fat, Foods Containing Sugar

Foods containing fat include margarine, butter, other spreading fats and low-fat spreads, cooking oils, oil-based salad dressings, mayonnaise, cream, chocolate, crisps, biscuits, pastries, cake, puddings, ice-cream, rich sauces and gravies.

Foods containing sugar include soft drinks, sweets, jam and sugar as well as foods such as cake, puddings, biscuits, pastries and ice-cream.

Foods containing fat do contain important nutrients including essential fatty acids and fat-soluble vitamins, especially the antioxidant vitamin E, and so a small amount is needed in the diet.

Generally, high-fat foods should be limited as they are high in energy and eating large quantities can lead to excessive gains in body fat. A high intake of saturated fat can also increase cholesterol levels.

Mono unsaturated or polyunsaturated fat should be chosen instead where possible. Look out for products with less than 3g fat per 100g as these are low fat.

Foods containing a lot of sugar can be useful to top up carbohydrate requirements but should not be included in large quantities. The food group 'bread, other cereals and potatoes' should make up a substantial part of a hockey player's diet because of the greater need for carbohydrate. Fruit and dairy foods are also a useful source of carbohydrate.

What Should I Eat Before a Match?

Pre-Match Meal

This meal should be eaten about two hours before the match, although it could be between one and four hours. It should be high in carbohydrate, low in fat, low-to-moderate in protein but with a low amount of fibre if nerves send you running to the bathroom. Too much protein will slow down the movement of foods from the stomach and will make you feel uncomfortable. It should provide approximately 200–300g (7–10oz) carbohydrate.

Suitable foods would be:

- pasta with tomato-based sauce with chicken and vegetables or other low-fat sauce
- stir-fried noodles or rice with vegetables and lean meat, chicken or prawns

Players drinking and eating snacks during a training session.

- vegetable and chicken risotto
- cereal and milk and/or yoghurt
- porridge made with milk
- toast, muffins or crumpets with honey, jam or marmalade
- spaghetti in tomato sauce or baked beans (if not too high in fibre) on toast
- sandwiches with lean meat, tuna or salmon
- jacket potatoes with low-fat toppings such as baked beans, cottage cheese or low-fat soft cheese, tuna and sweetcorn
- bagels, baguettes or sandwiches with lean cold meat, tuna or salmon
- low-fat milk shakes or smoothies
- cereal bars or breakfast bars
- low-fat rice pudding or low-fat yoghurt
- bananas
- isotonic sports drinks.

Pre-Match Snack

You may find it beneficial to take a small carbohydrate snack 30–60 minutes before the match to top up blood glucose levels. This could include:

- fresh or dried fruit
- cereal bars
- fig rolls
- rice cakes
- fruit loaf or malt loaf
- scotch pancakes
- sports drinks
- low-fat rice pudding or low-fat yoghurt.

What Should I Eat After Training?

Effective recovery from training is crucial to prevent that mid-week slump in energy levels. Rapid replenishment of the glycogen stores used during training and competition is essential. This is particularly important if you are training every day or more than once a day.

When you finish training, you should aim to have a carbohydrate-rich food or drink within 30 minutes as the muscle can store carbohydrate as glycogen more efficiently during this time.

You should aim for 1–1.2g carbohydrate per kg of body weight, so usually this would be a minimum of 50g (2oz)

carbohydrate. This amount should be consumed within 30 minutes and then repeated after two hours until normal meal patterns are resumed.

This process is a must if you have less than eight hours between training sessions or events, but not so crucial if you have a day or more between intensive training sessions. However, it is important that you consume a meal or snack soon after the end of training.

It would also be beneficial if the recovery snack and/or drink contained some protein to facilitate the repair, growth and development of muscle tissue. Ideally the snack should provide approximately 10–20g (½–¾oz) protein and 50–100g (2–4oz) carbohydrate depending on body weight.

If recovery time before the next session is short, the type of carbohydrate consumed should ideally be one that is quickly absorbed into the bloodstream, that is, a high glycaemic index food.

The following are examples of recovery snacks all providing 50g (2oz) carbohydrate. They can be combined with each other for variety and to increase the amount of carbohydrate provided. For example 500ml fruit juice and one English muffin and jam provide 75g carbohydrate. Milk or yoghurt-based drinks are an excellent way of consuming protein after training.

Recovery Snacks Containing 50g Carbohydrate

- 650–800ml isotonic sports drink
- 500ml low-fat milkshake, such as Yazoo, Gulp, Friji, Duns River Nourishment Light For Goodness Shakes milkshake
- 500ml fruit juice
- 300ml carbohydrate or energy drinks, such as Lucozade Energy, or 500ml SIS PSP22 (50g powder mixed with 500ml water)
- 500ml fruit smoothie
- two large bananas
- three medium pieces fruit
- two Nutrigrain bars or twists

- two Rice Krispie squares
- two Frusli bars
- two crumpets or English muffins with jam
- three scotch pancakes
- two teacakes
- two hot cross buns
- one bagel
- two or three slices malt loaf
- two fruit scones
- a large bowl of breakfast cereal with skimmed milk
- 70g or 2tbs raisins or sultanas
- five dried dates or 100g dried apricots or five figs.

Recovery Snacks and Drinks
Providing approx
50g Carbohydrate and
10–20g Protein

- 500ml Friji milkshake (51g carbohydrate, 17g protein, 4.0g fat, 310kcal)
- 500ml Breaktime milkshake (45.5g carbohydrate, 16.5g protein, 0.5g fat, 255kcal)
- 500ml For Goodness Shakes banana flavour milkshake (46g carbohydrate, 16.4g protein, 1.5g fat, 248kcal)
- 500ml strawberry Gulp (49g carbohydrate, 19g protein, 5g fat, 315kcal)
- 500ml semi-skimmed milk plus one cereal bar, such as Frusli (46.3g carbohydrate, 18.5g protein, 4.8g fat, 297kcal)
- 420g can Nourishment Light (48g carbohydrate, 23g protein, 3.8g fat, 319kcal)
- Homemade fruit smoothie with 150g yoghurt, 25ml fruit juice, one banana plus 3tbs skimmed milk powder (approx 65g carbohydrate, 20g protein, 300kcal, 2g fat)
- one round sandwiches (thick sliced bread) with low-fat spread and tuna, chicken, meat or cottage cheese plus one piece fruit (approx. 400kcal, 64g carbohydrate, 22g protein, 9g fat)
- 200g low-fat yoghurt plus cereal bar and banana (61.5g carbohydrate, 12g protein, 4.8g fat, 331kcal)

Add in cereal bars, sports drinks, bananas, dried fruits and so on to add more carbohydrate to match your needs.

Fluid and Hydration

Fluids play a vital role in maintaining body functions and make up 66 per cent of body weight. Fluid is required for the transport of vital nutrients around the body, removal of waste products, digestion and absorption of food and the maintenance of body temperature.

During any type of physical activity, heat is produced and lost from the body by the evaporation of sweat. This fluid loss is linked to the need to maintain the body temperature within narrow limits. Dehydration can have serious negative effects on performance and so it is important to keep hydrated at all times by frequent drinking before, during and after exercise.

The Effects of Dehydration

- Exercise performance can be impaired by 10–20 per cent if a player is dehydrated by as little as 2 per cent of body weight.
- Fluid losses in excess of 3 per cent increase the risk of heat cramps, heat exhaustion or heat stroke.
- Dehydration can affect mental function, slowing reaction and response times and decision making skills, which are vital in team sports.

Keeping Hydrated

Fluid should be regularly replaced during exercise. Fluid ingestion during and before exercise helps to restore your blood volume to near pre-exercise levels and prevents the adverse effects of dehydration on muscle strength, endurance and coordination.

Thirst is not a good indicator that you need fluid. By the time you are thirsty, you have started to become dehydrated, so it is important to drink before you become thirsty. You should drink at least two cups of liquid two hours before you exercise. Beverages such as water, low-fat or skimmed milk or fruit juices can be consumed leading up to a training session or event. Avoid drinking carbonated drinks because they could give you a stomach ache while you're competing.

Hydration Tips for Youngsters

- Young players are more likely to consume more of a flavoured beverage than water.
- The colder the drink the more palatable.
- Ensure that at training sessions and at matches every child has a large, accessible drink bottle so that it is easy for them to drink.
- To combine with their training and match schedule, draw up a fluid intake schedule to ensure young players are well hydrated before they begin their activity.
- Encourage children to drink smaller volumes more frequently before and during exercise to minimize stomach discomfort.

GLOSSARY

This is a glossary of words and terms used in hockey. You may or may not find them in an English dictionary, and if you do, the definitions will probably be very different from the ones given here.

Aerial pass   A pass (of the ball with a stick) up in the air.

Ball carry position   The key positions to carry and/or dribble the ball, and move with the ball.

Ball manipulation   The ability to move the ball left, right, forward and back.

Behind square   A pass that is made on a backwards angle to the goal-line or halfway line.

Block tackle   A solid full tackle where you block the route the ball carrier was running on.

Channelling   Forcing the ball carrier to go into an area of the pitch by the line you take.

Clip hit   A hit with a shortened grip, which is mostly used when shooting.

Closing down   Restricting or closing down the area that the ball carrier has to work in.

ClubsFirst accreditation   Recognition that a club is a safe environment for youngsters to play the game.

Club–School Link   An agreement between local clubs and schools to deliver hockey.

Core skills   The basic skills that you need to play the game: moving with the ball, passing, evading and tackling.

Core stability   The inner physical muscular strength of a player.

Covering   A team action ensuring you always have more players in defence than the opposition have in attack.

Cross   A ball hit in to the centre from wide on the pitch.

Deception   Trying to make the opposition think you will do one thing whilst knowing you will do another.

Defender   A player mainly responsible for stopping the opposition scoring goals.

Defending   The act of protecting or defending the goal from the opposition.

Delay   A method of slowing down the opposition.

Depth   Using depth means making sure that you use all areas of the pitch, particularly its length.

Diamond pass   A drill practising moving and passing on angles.

Dribble lanes and lines of defence   Lines of defence usually run across the pitch and are staggered so that the player with the ball cannot beat all the opposition with one move or pass. Dribble lanes therefore run around these lines of defence.

Dribbling   Moving with the ball; a ball carry position.

Dummy tackle   Making the opposition think you will make a tackle while you intend to win the ball in another way.

Eliminate   To get the ball round or past the defending player, taking the ball with a dribble or a pass to a teammate.

Evading   The act of moving the ball away from the defenders, to prevent them taking the ball; this can be by dribbling or passing the ball.

Fake   Making the opposition think you are taking one action while taking another.

Flick   The action of lifting the ball in the air. The action has no backswing and the stick is placed under the ball at the start.

Forward   A player mainly responsible for scoring goals.

Free hit   A hit given to the team who did not break the rule after a foul has been made.

Getting ahead   Creating space and leading the decision making of a player in an attacking situation. Being ahead of the ball carrier is not enough, you must continue to work ahead or rotate behind the ball carrier to get free, or create space for the ball carrier.

Hitting   Striking the ball using a swinging movement of the stick towards the ball.

Indian dribble   A movement of the ball from right to left and vice versa whilst moving forward.

Indoor hockey   A game played in a sports hall, similar to the outdoor version but with no hitting allowed; the ball can be played off the side walls.

Inject/Injection   A method of sending the ball out at a penalty corner.

Jab/Jab Tackle   The first stage of the tackle, making the ball carrier slow down and get their eyes down.

Jump back/Tackle back   The stage in a tackle when as soon as the team in possession lose the ball they immediately respond and try to regain possession.

Logging   An action by the goalkeeper where they make a long barrier against the ball by lying on the floor.

Man-for-man defence   Each person being responsible for one member of the other team and preventing them from getting the ball.

Midfielder   A player linking the forwards and defenders.

Mini-hockey   A 7-a-side game for youngsters played on half a full-sized pitch.

On the wing   Playing on an area down the side of the pitch.

Open stick   Playing the ball when it is on the right-hand side of the player.

Outlet   The direction the ball can be sent from deep defence.

Pass square   A pass that is made parallel to the goal-line or halfway line.

Pathways and channels   These are lines of play that are always drawn in relation to the goal that the players are moving towards.

Penalty corner A free hit given for a foul inside the shooting area in favour of the attack. Five defenders are allowed to stand behind the goal-line whilst the attackers start around the circle edge.

Penalty stroke A free hit given for a deliberate foul inside the shooting area, or a foul that would have stopped a certain goal.

Penetration The act of attacking the opposition lines of play and getting into areas of effect.

Physiologist A person responsible for writing fitness programmes for hockey players.

Physiotherapist A trained person responsible for dealing with any injuries to hockey players.

Player pathway The route for improving players, including schools, clubs and representative hockey.

Pointing at pressure Ensuring that you are dribbling the ball towards the space around the defending player, to enable the ball carrier to eliminate on outside or inside with a pass or dribble.

Posting up An action whereby a player not in possession of the ball, and ahead of the ball carrier, makes a run towards the ball carrier to offer themselves for a pass.

Post player The defensive player responsible for covering the goal-line by the side of the post at a penalty corner.

Pressing A team action to try to win the ball in defence by keeping the opposition in one area and with few options of passing or moving the ball.

Protecting the ball Carrying the ball away from the opposition so that they cannot steal it.

Pushing Moving the ball along the ground by using a pushing action: both the stick and ball are in contact with the

ground during the pushing action. The ball and stick stay in contact, so if you can hear a noise you are not pushing the ball.

Quicksticks A 4-a-side game for primary school children, which will introduce them to hockey.

Receiving Collecting the ball from a teammate preferably while in flow. Try to avoid standing still to receive, looking to roll out from the defending player where appropriate.

Rehabilitation The period after injury before a player is fit enough to play a game of hockey.

Representative honours These honours have traditionally represented county, regional and national teams.

Reverse hit A hit from the left-hand side of the body with the stick turned over in a reverse position.

Reverse stick The use of the stick on the left-hand side of the player.

Scanning/Pre-scanning The action of looking at the space available either for a pass or in which you as a player can travel with the ball.

Scoop Similar to a flick but slower to execute as the ball is taken over to the left-hand side of the body, and the ball is propelled into the air.

Screening The ability to use a teammate to act as a screen to the opposition, behind which you can receive or move for the ball.

Sideline hit A re-start hit used when the ball goes out of the pitch area.

Slalom Moving to the left and right around cones or opposition.

Slapping Striking the ball using a sweeping movement of the stick towards the ball, often with the stick head in contact with the ground during the backswing and follow-through; also referred to as a sweep.

Smothering Where the goalkeeper uses their whole body to prevent the ball from going into goal, and lies sideways on the ground to provide a long barrier.

Stance Body position.

Square To the left and right of the player and parallel with the endlines.

Systems of play Methods of placing team players in roles on the pitch.

Three-man weave A routine of passing and player movement down the pitch.

Tip-tapping The sound of the stick on the ball during a lazy way of dribbling; the ball carrier takes their stick off the ball and has to keep reconnecting with the ball making a tapping sound.

Trap/Trapper A method of controlling the ball at a penalty corner before the striker shoots.

Turnover When the opposition get the ball off your team and then have possession of it.

V drag A evasion skill used to move the ball to avoid the opposition.

Vision and scanning Practises whereby a player looks up while moving around the pitch, either with or without the ball. Also, the ability to see the opposition and which direction they are moving around the pitch.

Wall pass A pass that is given straight back to you as in the action of sending a ball at the wall.

Winger A wide attacking player, a forward.

Zonal defence A method of defence whereby each team member takes responsibility for an area of the pitch and prevents the opposition from going into that area.

3D skills Skills that take in the use of height, that is, passing the ball into the air as well as on the ground.

USEFUL ADDRESSES

England Hockey
The National Hockey Stadium
Silbury Boulevard
Milton Keynes
MK9 1HA
www.englandhockey.co.uk

European Hockey Federation
Avenue des Arts 1–2
1210 Brussels
Belgium
www.eurohockey.org

Great Britain Hockey Ltd
Bisham Abbey NSC
Marlow
Buckinghamshire
SL7 1RR
www.greatbritainhockey.co.uk

International Hockey Federation
Residence du Parc
Rue du Valentin 61
1004 Lausanne
Switzerland
www.worldhockey.org

Scottish Hockey
589 Lanark Road
Edinburgh
EH14 5DA
www.scottish-hockey.org.uk

Welsh Hockey Union
Severn House
Station Terrace
Ely
Cardiff
CF5 4AA
www.welsh-hockey.co.uk

Hockey Australia
Level 1
433–435 South Road
Bentleigh
Victoria 3204
www.hockey.org.au

Hockey New Zealand
PO Box 24-024
Royal Oak
Auckland 1345
www.hockeynz.co.nz

Indian Hockey Federation
8/40 South Patel Nagar
New Delhi – 110 008
Tel: 011-2584 9794, 011-2584 3410
Fax: 011-2584 2475
www.indiahockey.org

US Field Hockey Association
1 Olympic Plaza
Colorado Springs
CO 80909
www.usfieldhockey.com

Field Hockey Canada
Hockey sur gazon Canada
240-1101 Prince of Wales Drive
Ottawa, Ontario
Canada, K2C 3W7
www.fieldhockey.ca

South African Hockey Association
PO Box 11573
Hatfield, Pretoria 0028
www.sahockey.co.za

OPRO
Unit 1, A1M Business Centre
151 Dixon's Hill Road
Welham Green
Hatfield
Herts
AL9 7JE
www.opro.com

INDEX